Europe: Civilizations Clashing

Piotr Jaroszyński/Lindael Rolstone

Europe: Civilizations Clashing

From Athens to the European Union

PETER LANG

**Bibliographic Information published by the
Deutsche Nationalbibliothek**
The Deutsche Nationalbibliothek lists this publication in the Deutsche
Nationalbibliografie; detailed bibliographic data is available online at
http://dnb.d-nb.de.

Library of Congress Cataloging-in-Publication Data
A CIP catalog record for this book has been applied for at the
Library of Congress.

This publication was financially supported by the John Paul II Catholic
University of Lublin.

Cover illustration: © Shutterstock.com/PNIK

ISBN 978-3-631-76453-4 (Print)
E-ISBN 978-3-631-79986-4 (E-PDF)
E-ISBN 978-3-631-79987-1 (EPUB)
E-ISBN 978-3-631-79988-8 (MOBI)
DOI 10.3726/b16055

© Peter Lang GmbH
Internationaler Verlag der Wissenschaften
Berlin 2019
All rights reserved.

Peter Lang – Berlin · Bern · Bruxelles · New York · Oxford · Warszawa · Wien

This publication has been peer reviewed.

www.peterlang.com

Acknowledgements

The authors thank the John Paul II Catholic University of Lublin, Poland, for their generous contribution to this project.

We thank our publisher, Peter Lang and his assistants.

The authors thank our mutual friend, Jolanta Dawa, for connecting the two authors. She is a Canadian with a previous Polish background. The authors, who, incidentally, had not met at the time of book publication, collaborated efficiently through technology.

The authors thank Janice Yeaman, a Canadian, who offered some insights into the protestant perspective. Many of her questions were answered and inserted into the body of the text. Some of her insights and feedback concerning a protestant perspective were also incorporated into the text.

The authors, Professor Jaroszyński and Lindael Rolstone, thank each other, for an enjoyable few years as we collaborated together across the continents and time zones through email communication. We anticipate this project to elicit respectful comments, agreements and disagreements, and questions, as our readers consider what is written in this text. These comments could be the subject of a future book and collaboration, of which both authors would welcome.

Contents

Introduction

Europe's Identity Shaped Through Clashes in Europe's History

European identity was formed throughout the generations, largely because of major value clashes occurring throughout time. Europe has been a battlefield. Clashes over Europe involved geography, culture, philosophy, religion, essential values, practices of living out life... the list is ongoing. Europe, and European identity, was formed, evolved and developed because of, and in spite of these clashes between civilizations. Evaluating and examining these European clashes were, and continues to be, extremely complicated and controversial. Because these clashes are and were multifaceted, European Identity can only be evaluated through careful scrutiny of emerging etymological, geographical, political, historical, cultural, religious, civilizational and ideological aspects. Europe's beginnings may include the inception of geographical maps, myths about gods and goddesses, the impact of inhabitants of Europe and conquerors, these all influenced the development of Europeanism cultural development. (Chapter 1)

This work addresses a select portion of European issues and concepts that have emerged in the course of history. The dissention over Europe continues into the present day. Clashes now involve the European Union. This discord is explained. The dispute is discussed in the context of Europe's past, present, and potential future. The history of Europe's civilization forms a context in making evaluations about the present.

Within the successive concepts of Europe, central characteristic features emerge. These traits form the basis of who and what Europe is and what it stands for. These central features emerge in opposition to non-European cultures or civilizations. In our current era, there is an internal dispute over Europe from within Europe. One thing is certain: Europe is not a ready category that can be indisputably referenced.

Europe has distinctive features, to be reached, uncovered and saved. Europe is not a fluid category that may be arbitrarily shaped. European features enrich the spectrum of cultures and civilizations of the world, and this is because they have a universal, trans-European value.

Culture, Religion, and Science Shaping Europe's History

European history points to three main divergent concepts of Europe, which appear in the context of clashes grounded in civilization. Dominant themes emerge, those of culture, religion, and science. The field of impact is variable and the European nations, which are involved, differ in their own unique ways.

In the most ancient times, one clash, the first concept of Europe, included the clash between the Greeks and Persians. The Greek philosophers of that time period referred to their conflict with Persia as being a clash between Europe and Asia. (Chapter 2)

Christianity was introduced into the Greek culture, and is discussed in terms of the principles of Europe's culture and history. Christianity clashes within itself, leading to the Protestant Reformation. Christianity and Islam meeting head-on introduce the second idea. As contrasted with the peaceful philosophy of Christians, Islam had a hostile attitude towards Christians, and attempted to take Europe by force. (Chapter 3) Historically, Europe under Christianity promoted the concept of equality among people, and intellectual growth and progress. It served to unite and bond the people throughout Europe. (Chapter 4) Equality, freedom and Justice were promoted in the political dimension, emphasizing a freedom that focused upon the common good. (Chapter 5)

The third concept resulted from the European cultures intermingling with the cultures of the newly discovered people who inhabited other continents. Clashes ensued.

Confrontations shaped Europe as a phenomenon diversified in terms of both civilization and geography. European culture and civilization are unique when considered in the context of three central clashes, the Greeks and the Persians, Christianity clashing within itself and with Islam, and cultures intermingling with those from other continents.

As a result of meeting of the three afore mentioned historical concepts, three new ideas of Europe emerge. These took the form of internal conflicts. The first was opposition against the Greek Europe. During the Christian era, conflict between Catholics and Protestants emerged. Lastly, a post-Christian age emerged, a modern age, termed the Enlightenment.

Other clashes and turning points continued throughout history. The loss of Christian values and behavior promoting peace, forgiveness and tolerance, led to the rise of Nazism, Fascism, Socialism, and Communism. (Chapter 6) Although some initial aims of each of these "isms" may have been praiseworthy, the actual outcome was nothing short of horror.

To many, Europe means one of three things, each leading to a revolution of sorts. When one considers Europe by definition, one may be referring to Greece, Christianity, or Enlightenment.

The latest revolution began with the European Union (EU). The ideals of the Union that were initially formulated through the leaders of various European countries, included fellowship, peaceful human relationships and the valuing of all human life. It was hoped that these values would inevitably lead to world peace. (Chapter 6) As time progressed, these aims have been replaced with other less noble ones.

The change in Europe through the Union, has been subtle, and to the casual observer, may go unnoticed. It is essential that these changes not go unnoticed. It is essential that people, you, become educated regarding what is happening. Examine the past, be alert in the present, and be attentive to what could transpire in the future.

The current project, the European Union, aims to dismantle Europe's culture. It rejects Europe through Anti-Hellenism (anti ancient Greece), Anti-Christianism (anti-Christian religion), and Anti-nationalism (rejecting Enlightenment). (Chapter 7) These concepts will be expanded upon as we move through this book. Briefly, there exists a planned and deliberate strategy to create a new notion of Europe. Policies have been implemented and are meant to contradict the old concepts of Europe, to turn Europe into something that may not be admirable. The history or reality of European heritage, and the concept about what makes Europe to be uniquely Europe, is being rejected in favor of a wave of new thinking and practice. That is their hallmark. Europe is ceasing to be Europe. Tools for this project are used and implemented centrally. These tools are available primarily by means of the state and international organizations, achieved by means of this European Union. (Chapters 7 and 8)

Challenges in Compiling and Presenting this Information

Factors influencing the development and maintenance of European culture were multifaceted.

Providing a concise description of these factors was challenging.

Some information is not normally reported by mainstream media or political forces, and the authors aspired to provide the reader with this relevant information. In order to discourse about Europe accurately, simplifications and manipulations, based upon the ahistorical and unilateral and concept of Europe, must be guarded against. Political forces may use the European Union as a tool to satisfy media or ideological aims. In reality, in their discourse to the public, the facts as presented by the Union may not be accurate or complete. This created the first challenge to overcome.

The second challenge in writing this book involved the large time span over which this book covers. Europe's history spanned centuries. When writing about a Europe that spans such a large period of time, a Europe rich with so much diversion in its history, the focus was narrowed. The intent is to capture the inner logic of Europe, why and how Europe evolved. Some details have been left out or discussed with the barest of detail, in order to not put the reader aside from the main current of thought. The questions of essential differences which appeared in Europe, and which had influence upon the idea of Europe, are the focus of this discourse. Another challenge was the use of correct words and terminology. It is now almost impossible to find a method of presenting information in a "politically correct' manner. The English language is not traditionally gender neutral. Finding a method to refer to man, woman, human beings, became challenging. The intent was to be respectful, and yet maintain the true meaning of the words used in context. Some of the European history involved Christian biblical text, in which the word "MAN" was used. Much research and discussion about proper terminology to use in this book ensued. Because it became of such interest to the authors, some of the highlights of our research are shared with the reader. A sentence from the Christian biblical text, siting the book of Genesis, states that the Lord formed "MAN" out of the dust of the ground and every living thing from the clay of the earth.[1] In Genesis of

---

1   "then the Lord God formed man from the dust of the ground, and breathed into his nostrils the breath of life; and the man became a living being". Genesis 2:7: *New Revised Standard Version Bible, Catholic Edition (NRSVCE)*, copyright © 1989, 1993 the Division of Christian Education of the National Council of the Churches of Christ in the United States of America. Used by permission.

the bible, it states that God first created man (as a male - Adam) and then as a woman (female - Eve), male and female in his image".[2] The word "man" (Adam) has a double meaning. There is a play on the word of Adam. The Hebrew word "Adam" is a generic term meaning human being, and "adama" was the word to signify the ground. The archetypal human being is understood to be male (Adam). Sometimes, the word "MAN" involves an official English title, such as man in culture, and because of this, the word was left unchanged.[3] In some languages, traditionally in the English language, the word "MAN" has been used to refer to both the human person, and the male. In more modern times, in the English language, an attempt is being made to create changes in language that becomes gender respectful. In other languages, for example the Polish language, different words are used to refer to a man ("mężczyzna"), a woman ("kobieta") and for both man and woman, a human being ("człowiek").

All rights reserved: https://www.biblegateway.com/theNewRevisedStandardVe rsionBible/CatholicEdition (RESVCE).

2 "So God created man in his own image, in the image of God he created him; male and female he created them". Genesis 1:27 *New Revised Standard Version Bible, Catholic Edition (NRSVCE),* copyright © 1989, 1993 the Division of Christian Education of the National Council of the Churches of Christ in the United States of America. Used by permission. All rights reserved: https://www.biblegateway. com/theNewRevisedStandardVersionBible/CatholicEdition (RESVCE).

3 A fifth year seminarian student, Dominic Rosario, answered the question about *Man* versus gender neutral language, in the following way: The Hebrew word *adam* and the Greek *anthropos* are generic terms that can be gender neutralized into such terms as *person* or *human*. Such is in fact a faithful translation. There are, however, instances in the Bible when the Hebrew word *ish* and the Greek *aner* are used. These actually refer to the masculine gender and thus cannot be changed to a gender-neutral word without changing the original meaning of the word. The main reason it is wrong to gender neutralize these words, (that this seminarian found in his research) was not for theological reasons at all. It is for practical purposes. When translating a text, you keep it as close to the original as possible. This is especially true when it comes to pronouns, because changing a "he" to "they", or "you", can really change the meaning of a sentence. If the original Greek or Hebrew text uses a masculine word, it is best to translate it to the English equivalent. There are also theological reasons why we can't change "Son of Man" to "Son of human" (These go beyond the realm of this book).

The authors considered the use of "MAN" (woman) in order to be inclusive. The challenge was to avoid language which could become monotonous to a reader: man (woman) following political correctness. We used traditional language where the use of the word man could have the narrow meaning to the word (male), or MAN (human being) to represent the larger meaning of humanity. We the writers understand that even this is not adequate in our writing. For the purposes of this book, it was decided to use the politically correct terminology wherever possible, including man, (woman), person, human, and human being. When the word man needed to remain in order to keep the meaning of the translation intact, the word man was written as "MAN". Changing the word under the impression of political correctness would have caused problems with the historical texts being referred to.

Gender respectful and gender-neutral language has become so diverse and quickly changing, that it is difficult to keep abreast of the changes. Another challenge was finding a word in the English language to represent gender respectfulness. The authors understand that there are now over eighty words in English to represent gender. The usage of these words is well beyond the scope of this book.

The Circular versus the Linear Mind

The authors were fascinated by one of many literary differences between their respective cultures and languages. The reader may be interested in the way the mind is taught to read and express itself through different cultures, as we were. The Polish European mind processes information in a circular dimension, while the anglophone North American mind reads and absorbs information in a linear fashion. When reading in Polish, the main subject of the paragraph may be found in the middle of the paragraph. An anglophone reader reads a paragraph linearly, starting with the subject of the paragraph at the beginning, and summarized at the completion of the paragraph.

Professor P. Jaroszyński originally wrote a rough draft of this book in Polish, and then it was translated into English. A mutual and good friend of both authors connected the two in order to enhance readability for the anglophone reader. As the two authors collaborated, they discovered that a direct translation was difficult if not impossible for Lindael Rolstone to read. She struggled to find Professor P. Jaroszyński's message in the middle of each paragraph, and then re write the paragraph in order for the anglophone mind to comprehend the message. This work required many years of collaboration, yet enjoyable and challenging to both.

Finding an Appropriate Title

There were many possible appropriate book titles, it was difficult to determine the most concise and descriptive title. The European Union; World Peace or World Division; War and Conflict; Civilizations Clashing: from Athens to the European Union…. These would all be appropriate titles for this book. The European Union is a subject that has the world's attention due to current conflicts around the globe. In the historical reference, the Union is not central throughout the book, although historical events leading up to the formation of the Union are significant. All of the background information about the civilizations of Europe may put into context and explain what is happening now with the European Union. Will the Union be able to meet its objectives? Will the Union promote world peace, or instead, will it lead to disaster, war and conflict?

The Subject Matter of Some Parts of this Book

Christianity and Islam have similar and divergent views and required much precision in their discussion. Presenting Christianity in the context of Europe's history became a significant challenge. This book was designed to be a philosophical book, not a religious or apologetic one. Documenting the development of Christianity and Islam, and the relevant corresponding belief systems, was important to the development of Europe's culture. It was the authors' intent to present an objective discussion about these beliefs. Another challenge regarding Christianity was the different belief systems within the religion itself. With over 64,000 denominations of Christian religions, it became a challenge to discuss Christian thought. There are key concepts that define all Christians, and where possible this is what is alluded to. Where certain specific belief systems were mentioned, these are made clear, such as Catholics believe… or Protestants believe.There is a strong anti-Christian sentiment in much of the world today. This made approaching the subject difficult, but necessary. Christian attitudes and behaviors significantly shaped Europe's history.

The Books Readership

This is a book about Europe. Europe, the history and diversified cultures, gives it a special appeal. One could approach this book as an academic exercise. It is hoped that you the reader may find a personal appeal to this book. Whether you live, have lived, travelled in Europe, have ancestors from there, or are concerned about the world we live in, this book is for you. Issues facing the current Europe are worldwide and universal. Preserving culture, heritage, tradition, language, world peace and world harmony, are not issues isolated to Europe. These issues are of great magnitude and are global issues. Become involved in the geography and the formation of history and culture as you move through this book. History shapes the present. The future may move in two different directions. Where have we been in the world with our unique cultures, and where are we going? That is the question to ponder.

This is an academic book. The intent is to present information in a language that can be read and understood by those who do not specialize in the field of philosophy. Philosophy as a discipline can be confusing for those not versed in its specific nuances. As a philosophy book, there may be some parts of the book that may only be presented with the specific language of philosophy. Our intention was to not make this book too academic, allowing a wide range of intelligent readers the opportunity of enjoying the subject, as the authors do.

And Now, Let's Begin

Journey with us as we move through time. Explore how Europe was formed geographically. Investigate the development of culture beginning with classical Greece until the present. Journey with us as we explore the chaos and upheaval shaping culture. Probe the impact of faith upon civilization. Notice the political forces that challenged Europe throughout history. Lastly, move into our current cultural clash involving the European Union. Get ready for quite a journey.

I. Europe Beginning

The Word Europe: Etymology

The word "Europe" has no explicit semantic root, nor is it a Greek word.[4] In the Phoenician language the word was associated with the evening land. In the Assyrian language the word "ereb" or "irib" was linked with Western Asia, while the word "acou" denotes Eastern Asia. In the Greek Language, the word "erebennós" means dark and obscure.[5]

Europe may be connected most strongly with Greece because of its coastal position. Greece lies west on the coast of Asia, and includes Phoenicia, Assyria, and Greek colonies.

Mythology: Europe Began by Force or Seduction?

According to Greek Mythology, Europe could have begun through either seduction or through brute force. The first mythical account portrays Europe as being a victim, having been seduced by Asia.[6] The scene of the myth takes place on the coast of Asia, and occurs before the time of Moses, who biblically, probably existed in the fourteenth century B.C. (Moses was known to be the person who helped free the Israelites from the captivity of the Egyptians).[7]

In the second mythological account, Europe was acquired by force, through the god Zeus. The Greeks considered Zeus to be the most important of the gods. The story, like many other stories, involves a beautiful woman. It all began in Phoenicia, an ancient Semitic civilization that spread across the Mediterranean Sea between 1500 BC and 300 BC. According to legend, the story involved three main characters: the god Zeus; a Phoenician king

---

4 *Online Etymology Dictionary*: 26 May 2018 https://www.etymonline.com/word/Europe.
5 Jean Carpentier, "L'Europe, le mot et le space," in *Histoire de l'Europe*, ed. Jean Carpentier and François Lebrun (Paris: Édition du Seuil, 1992), p. 14; Pim den Boer, "Europe to 1914: the Making of an Idea," in *The History of the Idea of Europe*, ed. Kevin Wilson and Jan van der Dussen (London; New York: Routledge, 1995), p. 15.
6 There were other myths regarding Europe, Carpentier, *Histoire de l'Europe*, p. 14.
7 The full account of the Exodus of the Israelites from Egypt may be found in the Christian bible, Exodus 14: 10–30.

named Agenor; and one of his most beautiful daughters. When Zeus saw the beautiful girl dancing with her sisters at the seashore near Tyre, her beauty captivated him. He fell instantly in love with her. Zeus developed a ruse to acquire his love. He planned to kidnap her. Zeus took the form of a bull. The curious girl fell for his trap. This beautiful young girl, hoping for a ride along the beach, mounted Zeus, – the bull. Once Zeus had the girl, he jumped into the water and travelled to Crete by the sea. The girl's shrill cries were to no avail. Her father and brothers were unsuccessful in their attempts to regain her. The girl, kidnapped by Zeus, was named Europe.[8] Legend came to life. Europe, by name, has now appeared in the Greek language.

Mythological stories about Europe have elicited many explanations and interpretations. The myth involving the god Zeus and the king's daughter is the most prevalent: The first: a god took the form of a bull to seduce an innocent victim. The second interpretation utilizes the symbol of a bull to represent power. A god through brute force and power acquired Europe. Europe became the victim of progress.

Christianity and a Supreme God

Christian Theologians explain Europe's beginnings as inspired and managed through a supreme God, who created heaven and earth[9] and every living thing from the clay of the earth.[10]

---

8   Robert Graves, *The Greek Myths* (Baltimore: Penguine Books, 1955), pp. 58–9; Luke Roman and Monica Roman, *Encyclopedia of Greek and Roman Mythology* (New York: Infobase Publishing, 2010), pp. 167–9. "This myth about the abduction of Europe was taken over by the Romans who began to reflect these myths in their painting (Pompeii), in sculpture, and in poetry (Ovidius, *Metamorphoses*, II, 837), Then it was included in the medieval and modern culture." *History of the Idea of Europe*, p. 14. Greek poet Moschus (second century BC) wrote the poem entitled *Europe*: 2 May 2018 http://www.theoi.com/Text/Moschus.html.

9   « In the beginning God created the heavens and the earth". Genesis 1:1. *New Revised Standard Version Bible, Catholic Edition (NRSVCE),* copyright © 1989, 1993 the Division of Christian Education of the National Council of the Churches of Christ in the United States of America. Used by permission. All rights reserved: https://www.biblegateway.com/theNewRevisedStandardVersio nBible/CatholicEdition (RESVCE).

10   "So out of the ground the Lord God formed every beast of the field and every bird of the air" Genesis 2:19: *New Revised Standard Version Bible, Catholic Edition*

Early Christian theologians, St. Jerome (347–420 A.D., priest, histo-rian), and St Ambrose (340–397 A.D., bishop of Milan, Roman governor), sited a biblical account to describe the formation of the continent of Europe. Biblically, Noah, in about 4000 BC, at the direction of a supreme God, built an ark. Noah and his family, with two by two of every kind of species, lived in this ark for approximately one year. By building and living in an ark, Noah's family was saved from a flood that would have eliminated the human race, and caused the extinction of life on earth.[11] Noah was thought to have had three sons, named Japheth, Shem and Ham. Japheth is the son described as being the ancestor to the European people.

(NRSVCE), copyright © 1989, 1993 the Division of Christian Education of the National Council of the Churches of Christ in the United States of America. Used by permission. All rights reserved: https://www.biblegateway.com/theNewRevisedStandardVersionBible/CatholicEdition (RESVCE)

11 "For behold, I will bring a flood of waters upon the earth, to destroy all flesh in which is the breath of life from under heaven; everything that is on the earth shall die". "Genesis 6:17:
"Then the Lord said to Noah, 'Go into the ark, you and all your household, for I have seen that you alone are righteous before me in this generation. [2] Take with you seven pairs of all clean animals, the male and its mate; and a pair of the animals that are not clean, the male and its mate; [3] and seven pairs of the birds of the air also, male and female, to keep their kind alive on the face of all the earth. [4] For in seven days I will send rain on the earth for forty days and forty nights; and every living thing that I have made I will blot out from the face of the ground.' [5] And Noah did all that the Lord had commanded him". (Genesis 7:1–5).
"[15] Then God said to Noah, [16] 'Go out of the ark, you and your wife, and your sons and your sons' wives with you. [17] Bring out with you every living thing that is with you of all flesh—birds and animals and every creeping thing that creeps on the earth—so that they may abound on the earth, and be fruitful and multiply on the earth.' [18] So Noah went out with his sons and his wife and his sons' wives. [19] And every animal, every creeping thing, and every bird, everything that moves on the earth, went out of the ark by families. (Genesis 8:15–19)
New Revised Standard Version Bible, Catholic Edition (NRSVCE), copyright © 1989, 1993 the Division of Christian Education of the National Council of the Churches of Christ in the United States of America. Used by permission. All rights reserved: https://www.biblegateway.com/theNewRevisedStandardVersionBible/CatholicEdition (RESVCE).

Mythology, Judaism, and Christianity

Greek mythology, Judaism, and later Christianity, shared commonalities in their explanations of Europe's inception, to the point that the stories at some moment in time became linked. One correlation was made between Noah's son, the biblical figure Japheth, and the mythical titans of the Greeks.

The Greeks thought the titans and titanesses were immortal divine beings. These divine beings were believed to be children of Gaia (Mother Earth), and Uranus (Father Sky). Gaia and Uranus served to unite heaven and earth. They were considered to be gods and goddesses of incredible strength.

Uranus and Gaia were thought to have had twelve children, six boys and six girls. One of their sons was named Iapetus. He was an important titan in mythology. Iapetus was the Greek God of fire, a master craftsman, and the creator of mortals. Iapetus was the father of Prometheus. Prometheus was the god who was credited for creating humans from clay. Connections were made at some point historically, between the mythological figure, Iapetus, and the biblical figure Japheth (Noah's son). These varying interpretations about Europe's inception generated a peculiar religious and mythological mixture to explain Europe's creation.[12]

Europe's Historical Geography

A geographical history of Europe and European borders, changeable and fluid, characterized Europe. The word continent stems from Latin[13] and denotes a large but limited area of land[14] surrounded by ocean waters. Thus, a continent is a huge island.

The image of the ancient world was comprised of three continents: Europe, Asia and Africa. It was believed that Asia occupied half of the world, while Africa and Europe each occupied one quarter.[15] In terms of location, Europe was to the north, Africa to the south, and Asia to the east. The Mediterranean Sea separated Europe from Africa. Three bodies of water,

---

12 Carpentier, *Histoire de l'Europe*, pp. 14–5.
13 Latin: *contineo, – ere.*
14 Greek – *épeiros.*
15 Carpentier, *Histoire de l'Europe*, p. 14.

the Don River, the Sea of Azov, and the Black Sea, separated Asia from Europe. The West of Europe was separated from Africa by mountains on either side. These mountains were named the Pillars of Hercules.[16] A narrow opening between these mountains was called the strait of Gibraltar.

In about 750 BC, when the classic literary genius Homer was composing poems, Europe was comprised of only two areas: Greece proper and Thrace. Trace was located to the south. Asia encompassed primarily Asia Minor. Both Europe and Asia were relatively small at that time. Europe was separated from Asia by three natural barriers of water, the Aegean Sea, the Dardanelles Lake, and Nea Propontida, which is in the central part of Macedonia in Greece. This body of water is now known as the Sea of Marmara.

In the eighth century before Christ, the process of intensive Greek colonization and the development of trade began. Ancient Greece began to have an influence upon the world. By the year 522 B.C., the word "Europe" still referred only to the Northern part of Greece.[17] Greek mythology continued to be rich and thriving. One popular myth involved Apollo (Asclepius), a good and helpful god. His story is as follows: Apollo travelled throughout Greece in search of the ideal place to position his temple. Once he had found and secured his temple, the god would communicate, through a priest or priestess, an oracle to his people. The oracle was a message or advice, usually wise and mysterious. The god Apollo provided the remedy for curing people who were poisoned by serpents. Apollo was thought to have obtained this remedy by killing the serpent Pythia, who in turn had obtained the herb against poison from another serpent. The Homeric Hymn to Pythian, in 522 B.C., was a famous poem about the god Apollo and his oracle.

---

16 Cape Calpe - the Gibraltar, and Cape Abila – Ceuta.
17 "Telphousa, here I intend to build a beautiful temple/to be an oracle for men who will always/bring to me here unblemished hecatombs;/and as many as dwell on fertile Peloponnesos/and on Europe and throughout the sea-girt islands," "To Apollon." *The Homeric Hymns*, trans. Apostolos N. Athanassakis, (Baltimore and London: John Hopkins University Press, 2004), 247–251.

Christian tradition tells a similar story of a supreme God speaking to his people through his prophets."[18] The Bible tells a story about people being healed from snakebites through the directions given to a prophet."[19]

By the fifth century before Christ, according to the famous Herodotus map (approximately 440 B.C.), Europe had expanded in size. Europe occupied a landmass that was two times larger than Africa. Located on this map were three important countries, Asia, Libya (now known as Africa), and Europe.[20] Europe at that time occupied the land north of the Mediterranean Sea, the Black Sea, and the Caspian Sea.

Strabo, a Greek geographer living one century before Christ, expanded the map of Europe. According to his map, Europe had expanded to include Spain, Gaul, Britain, Ireland, the Isle of Tule, Italy, Sicily, and the Balkan Peninsula. The Balkan Peninsula included Thrace, Macedonia, Epirus and the islands in the Aegean Sea.

Moving into the first century A.D., Europe was either relatively small, or quite large, dependent upon whether the Pliny map, or the Claudius Ptolemy map, is referred to. The information portrayed on each of these two maps conflicted with each other. Roman geographer Pliny the Elder maintained that Europe was larger in size than Asia and Africa.[21] According to the Claudius Ptolemy map (about 170 A.D.) Europe was quite small in

---

18 And the Lord said to Moses, "Lo, I am coming to you in a thick cloud, that the people may hear when I speak with you, and may also believe you for ever." Exodus 19:9. *New Revised Standard Version Bible, Catholic Edition (NRSVCE),* copyright © 1989, 1993 the Division of Christian Education of the National Council of the Churches of Christ in the United States of America. Used by permission. All rights reserved: https://www.biblegateway.com/theNe wRevisedStandardVersionBible/CatholicEdition (RESVCE).

19 "And the Lord said to Moses, "Make a fiery serpent, and set it on a pole; and every one who is bitten, when he sees it, shall live."". Numbers 21:8. *New Revised Standard Version Bible, Catholic Edition (NRSVCE),* copyright © 1989, 1993 the Division of Christian Education of the National Council of the Churches of Christ in the United States of America. Used by permission. All rights reserved: https://www.biblegateway.com/theNewRevisedStandardVersio nBible/CatholicEdition (RESVCE).

20 *450 B.C. – The World According to Herodotus.* 2 May 2018: https://www. awesomestories.com/asset/view/450-B.C.-The-World-According-to-Herodotus.

21 Boer, Europe, pp. 15–7, 29–32.

comparison with Africa and Asia. Africa included Libya and Ethiopia, and was slightly larger than Asia.

By the sixth century, Europe had expanded to include the lands lying north of the Mediterranean Sea. The River Don constituted a natural boundary.

By the middle Ages, a new image of Europe emerged, thanks to Isidore of Seville (approximately 570–636 B.C.), an author of the popular work entitled Etymologies.[22] His image of Europe was of one continent, reaching the Atlantic Ocean from the West, and the Don River from the East.

By the beginning of the eighteenth century, borders expanded to the East and the South of Europe. The Eastern border of Europe expanded beyond the river Don, in the direction of the Volga River and the Ural Mountains (Ph. J. von Strahlenberg, 1725 A.D.).[23] A newly discovered depression in the southeast, (P.S. Pallas, 1773 A.D.) in the area of the Kuma and Manych Rivers, became the natural border between Europe and Asia. As we move forward in time to the present, European borders

---

22 "ii. The globe (De orbe) 1. The globe (orbis) derives its name from the round-ness of the circle, because it resembles a wheel; hence a small wheel is called a 'small disk' (orbiculus). 1. Indeed, the Ocean that flows around it on all sides encompasses its furthest reaches in a circle. It is divided into three parts, one of which is called Asia, the second Europe, the third Africa. 2. The ancients did not divide the three parts of the globe equally, for Asia extends from south to north in the east, but Europe from the north to the west, Africa from the west to the south. 3. Whence it is clear that two of them, Europe and Africa, occupy half of the globe, Asia the other half by itself. But the former pair are divided into two regions, because from the Ocean the Mediterranean enters in between them and separates them. Wherefore, if you divide the globe into two parts, the east and the west, Asia will be in one, Europe and Africa in the other." Isidore of Seville, Etymologies, Stephen A. Barney, W. J. Lewis, J. A. Beach, Oliver Berghof (Cambridge: Cambridge University Press, 2006), Book XIV, II, 1–2. https://sfponline.org/Uploads/2002/st%20isidore%20in%20english.pdf: 11 November 2018.
II. DE ORBE. [1] [a latin translation may be found at: Isidori Hispalensis episcopi Etymologiarum sive originum libri XX. 2 May 2018: http://www.thelatinlibrary.com/isidore/14.shtml.
23 Probably it was inspired by Wasilij. N. Tatiszczew. Wikipedia, Boundaries between Continents: 2 May 2018 http://en.wikipedia.org/wiki/Boundaries_between_continents.

may be classified with two distinct versions. The first version utilizes the Caucasus Mountains in Europe, forming a natural border between Russia, Georgia, and Azerbaijan. When the Eastern border is considered to extend behind the Ural Mountains, the Ural Mountains are included in maps of Europe.[24]

The second accepted version locates the Caucasus Mountains in Asia, and assumes the border crosses the Kuma-Manych Depression. In both of these versions, Europe now stretches to the east to the Ural Mountains and to the Caucasus. Europe is basically a peninsula or a subcontinent of the Asian continent like India as a subcontinent of Asia.[25] Continental Europe of today has doubled in size. Still, when compared with other continents, the size of Europe is unimpressive, occupying only approximately 7 % of the total land area of the world.

To best understand Europe, one must consider its culture and civilization, as well as its geographical history.[26] Europeanism includes a mix of cultures and political factions. These cultures and political factions continually attempt to dethrone Europe, and bring into question its continental identity.

---

24 In *Wikipedia* one can read that "in 1958, the Soviet Geographical Society formally recommended that the boundary between the Europe and Asia to be drawn in textbooks stretching from Baydaratskaya Bay, on the Kara Sea, along the eastern foot of Ural Mountains, then following the Ural River until the Mugodzhar Hills, and then to the Emba River; and the Kuma–Manych Depression. This would place the Caucasus entirely in Asia and the Urals entirely in Europe. However, most geographers in the Soviet Union favored the boundary to run along the Caucasus crest, which became the standard convention in the latter 20th century. The Kuma–Manych boundary did remain and was portrayed in some 20th-century maps." *Boundaries*, https://en.wikipedia.org/wiki/Boundaries_between_continents, Geography seems to be under political pressure in the times of Peter the Great and Soviet Russia as well.

25 Rocco Buttiglione, Jarosław Merecki, *Europa jako pojęcie filozoficzne, [Europe as a Philosophical Concept]* (Lublin: Towarzystwo Naukowe KUL, 1996), p. 31.

26 Edgar Morin, as quoted by Giovanni Reale, says that the essence of Europeanism is based more on a specific spirit than on geography. G. Reale, *Raíces culturales y espirituales de Europa. Por un renacimiento de 'hombre europeo'*, trans. Maria Pons Irazazábal, (Madrid: Herder Editorial, 2005), p. 5.

Europe's Developing Culture

The development of Europeanism and Culture is elusive, it is difficult to determine and define. A variety of factors need to be considered in order to determine what a European culture might be, what part of the culture may be unique to Europe, and what cultures may be shared with other countries and peoples. Let's examine through time how culture may have been influenced and formed in Europe.

The concept of a European culture as being European is of late origin. A thread characteristic of the so-called European culture, also collectively called a Western culture, is searched for rather retrospectively.

The European culture, neither appeared in Europe in a geographical sense, nor was it limited to Europe.[27] Moreover, the process of Europeanization of the geographical Europe lasted until the end of the middle Ages. Large tracts of Europe already Europeanized, gradually ceased to be culturally European. Notwithstanding, continental Europe, and the scope of the European culture, did not denote the same thing.

The discrepancy between geography and culture makes the concept of European culture so elusive, that it sparkles with different shades, and requires precision in an approach to understand it.

To outline some of the various means of determining a European culture, one may consider several factors, including: geographical division, the process of Europeanization, when and how the culture developed, what aspects of culture may continue to exist today, what parts of the culture are unique to Europe, and what parts are shared with other peoples.

Using the above criteria, many problems emerge when considering the development of a European culture. Europeanization of the geographical Europe lasted until the end of the middle Ages. In present times, a concept of a culture referred to as European does not coincide with geographical divisions. Moreover, a European culture neither appeared in Europe in a

---

27 Apart from Hellenism, European civilization and even a European idea of a man or a woman would be inconceivable. Nevertheless, Greek civilization itself was far from being European in a geographical sense. Christopher Dawson, *The Making of Europe. An Introduction to the History of European Unity* (Washington DC: The Catholic University of America Press, 2003), p. 16.

geographical sense, nor was it limited to Europe. Continental Europe, and the scope of the European culture, does not denote the same thing. Also, large tracts of Europe already Europeanized gradually ceased to be culturally European.

The Ionians, one of the four major Greek tribes who came from Europe, were one tribe who had a significant influence upon Greek culture. They first appeared in about 1100 B.C., forming colonies on the coasts of Asia Minor. Ionia was located in what is now present-day Turkey. The Ionic tribe was identified through their use of the Eastern Greek language, and by tradition. Philosophy curriculums included both the Milesian and the Ionian schools of thought. The Milesians focus of philosophy was upon nature, and the Ionians focused upon reason and thought.

Strife between the Persian empire and the Greeks was on going. When the Persians invaded and destroyed Ionic centers of Greek culture, the Greeks relocated to Great Greece, and to Greek colonies located in southern Italy and Sicily. Magna Graecia, a name which means "Great Greece", was the name given by the Romans to an area of southern Italy. Greek settlers, who, in the eighth century B.C., extensively populated these areas, brought with them their Hellenic civilization, having a lasting effect on the culture of these regions. The Italian Magna Graecia school of philosophy was known for its combination of philosophy and mysticism.

Geographically, European culture was born on the coasts of Asia Minor, not on the European continent. Distinct origins of the European culture date back to Homer, a Greek poet who lived about 750 B.C. Philosophers began appearing between the seventh and the fifth centuries before Christ. Thales of Miletus, was one great philosopher who lived between 624–547 B.C. He was the first person to base his explanation upon scientific philosophy instead of mythology.

In summary, between the eighth century B.C. and the fourth century B.C., the Western culture was the sphere of influence of the Greek culture. This exerted however, a very small geographical impact.

The range of influence of Greek culture began to grow not only in Europe, but also in Asia, because of the influence of an undefeated, influential, and successful military commander known as Alexander the Great, who lived between 356 B.C. and 323 B.C. He created one of the largest empires of the ancient world, stretching from Greece to north-western India. The Hellenic period developed. This period in history developed due to Greek influence. Cultural centers were located in Alexandria (Africa), Athens (Greece), and in Bactria (Asia). At the same time, the Greek culture influenced by the East, began to Orientalize, creating a movement from a Hellenic culture to a Hellenistic culture. Hellenic culture refers to ancient Greece or the Greeks of the classical period (776–323 B.C.). Hellenistic culture refers to the Greek civilization in the Mediterranean world from about 323 B.C. to about 30 B.C.

In consequence, a uniquely European culture became more and more difficult to define. In the meantime, Rome was developing into an Empire. This Roman Empire did not affect the whole of Europe. It did however gradually take over the Greek cultural heritage of the entire Mediterranean Basin, including the rivers Rhine and Danube to the North.

The Romans did not pay much attention to the notion of Europeanism. Instead, Rome had plans and ambitions to not only conquer Europe, but to master the whole world.[28] Virgil, an ancient Roman poet, referred to the disinterest of Romans regarding European culture, portrayed through the song of Anchises

> Let others better mold the running mass
> Of metals, and inform the breathing brass,
> And soften into flesh a marble face;
> Plead better at the bar; describe the skies,
> And when the stars descend, and when they rise.
> But, Rome, 'tis thine alone, with awful sway,
> To rule mankind, and make the world obey,
> Disposing peace and war by thy own majestic way;
> To tame the proud, the fetter'd slave to free:
> These are imperial arts, and worthy thee.[29]

Roman armies began by conquering the three coastal continents of the Mediterranean Basin: Europe, Asia and Africa. Through its successful conquests, Rome was gradually able to rule over the peoples of the whole

---

28 Francois Hartog, "Fondamenti greci dell'idea d'Europa," in: Idee di Europa. Attualità e fragilità di un progetto antico, ed. L. Canfora, Bari, 1997, p. 27.

29 Publius Vergilius Maro, *Aeneid*, VI, 847–854, trans. John Dryden. Perseus Digital Library: 3 May 2018 http://www.perseus.tufts.edu/hopper/text?doc=Pe rseus%3Atext%3A1999.02.0052%3Abook%3D6%3Acard%3D801.

world. Its position became so strong, that neither politicians nor writers felt the need to refer to Europe as the "Emblem of Rome". As Rome dominated Europe, it had a significant influence upon the developing civilization. The Roman culture incorporated elements of Greek, Celtic, German, and Latin[30] languages, into a western framework.[31]

Augustus became the first Roman emperor. He controlled the Roman Empire from 27 B.C. until his death in 14 A.D. The Roman culture preserved the essential elements of the western culture, and avoided an Egyptian Oriental influence, owing to the victory of Augustus at Actium.[32]

Rome did incorporate ideas taken from the Greek culture, and is credited for spreading the Greek culture and its ideals throughout Europe. In consequence, Rome, besides displaying aspirations to rule over Europe, constituted an important complement and expansion of many Greek achievements in their western dimension.[33]

---

30 Latinitatis.

31 It was the concept of Julius Caesar, thanks to his initiative, a major part of Europe is included into the western culture. Dawson, *Making of Europe*, pp. 17–8.

32 Dawson, *Making of Europe*, p. 19.

33 This role of Rome with regard to the Greek culture was underlined by the Greeks themselves, including Polybius and Strabo. Christopher Dawson, "Europe and the Seven Stages of Western Culture," in: *Christianity and European Culture. Selections from the Work of Christopher Dawson*, ed. Gerald J. Russello (Washington: Catholic University of America Press, 1998), p. 137.

II. Greece: Clashes, Politics, and Philosophical Thought

Greece and Persia Clashing

A well formed European culture, uniting in common interests, ideals, and values, was crystallized in Greece between the fifth and forth centuries B.C. The development of this common culture came about through centuries of development and upheaval. Dominant opposing forces involved the Greeks and the Asians. In terms of a cultured society, the Greeks considered the Asians to be barbarians. The significant beginning of a developed and distinguished culture most probably may be attributed to the cultured Greek people.

Two great Greek thinkers of the time, Hippocrates and Aristotle, expressed strong opinions supporting Greek cultural advancement and influence. Hippocrates was born about 460 B.C. and is reputed as being the father of modern medicine. Aristotle (384–322 B.C.) was an ancient Greek philosopher and scientist, who is accredited for developing the first comprehensive system of Western philosophy.

Hippocrates believed that there were inherent organic and mental differences between Asians and Greeks. He classified the Asians as being weak in spirit, passive, lacking in initiative and lacking in courage. He attributed these characteristics to the location in which these Asians lived. They lived in a location in which there was a single yearly season, monotonous climate, and unchanging temperature. Contrasting the personalities of the Asians, the people of Greece, were full of spiritual vitality, courage, and were inventive and active.[34] Hippocrates postulated that the people of Greece had qualities, personalities, and behaviors, which were different from the Asians, because they lived in a country that had changing seasons, weather conditions, climate, and temperatures.

---

34 Hippocrates, "Influences of Atmosphere, Water and Situation," in: *Greek Historical Thought from Homer to the Age of Heraclius*, trans. Arnold J. Toynbee (Boston: Beacon, 1950), p. 165. *The History of the Idea of Europe*, p. 16.

Aristotle classified Greeks as having qualities including intelligence, bravery, creativity, and a love of freedom.[35] He considered the Asians and Northern Europeans to be barbarians. He believed that the Asians were neither smart nor brave, and lacked the love of freedom. Aristotle postulated that the northern Europeans (i.e. geographic Europeans), were bold but not clever. Aristotle did acknowledge that the Asians were creative, a trait that he postulated would not necessarily be of use to them. Because of the negative characteristics that he attributed to the Asians, he believed they could succumb to despotism, a form of government which rules with absolute power.

Self-Awareness and Culture

The Greeks developed laws to protect fundamental human rights, and through these laws they clearly defined human responsibilities that were required of them while living in a Greek state.

By the end of the fifth century B.C., Greek culture began to be formed into some key components, including law, human rights, and human responsibilities. Greek laws were developed, and aimed to serve and to protect individuals, valuing the person more than the state. Essential fundamental human rights were outlined. These rights included liberty, privacy, justice, the right to develop personal talents, and the right to live according to personal preferences. Individual responsibilities included obeying laws, and serving and protecting one's country.

Pericles (495–429 B.C.), was influential in Greek development. He was a politician and a military general during the Persian[36] and Peloponnesian[37] wars. Pericles promoted the arts and literature. Through his leadership, Athens became the educational and cultural center of the ancient Greek

---

35 Aristotle, *Politics*, trans. Benijamin Jowett, VII, 1: 3 May 2018 http://classics.mit.edu/Aristotle/politics.7.seven.html.

36 **The Persian Wars**, (492–449 B.C.), were fought between Greek States and Persia. Greece triumphed, allowing Greek culture and political structure to survive long after the Persian Empire fell. https://www.britannica.com.

37 The **Peloponnesian War**, (431–404 B.C.), was a war that may have been considered as the most monumental war up until that time. Most of the Greek world were involved. https://www.britannica.com.

world. Due to the influence of Pericles, freedom of expression and democracy developed and grew, becoming his legacy.

By the end of the late fifth century B.C, a public funeral was held in Greece to honor the soldiers who were killed at war. These public funerals became an established Athenian practice. Pericles is renowned for a funeral speech delivered following the First Peloponnesian War. The funeral speech was written and delivered with the intent of increasing the morale of a people at war, to glorify Athens, and to honor fallen soldiers. Pericles's speech provides a good description of the distinct Greek culture of the era.

Some scholars consider Pericles's funeral speech to be difficult to read and understand, due to its rhetorical speech, the specific choice of words used, and the elaborate speech. It is important, as it serves to illustrate the Greek idea of democracy. Because of its fame, and impact upon both Greece and future generations, Pericles's speech is referenced. Of the many translations of this speech, one English translation is as follows

"Our constitution does not copy the laws of neighboring states; we are rather a pattern to others than imitators ourselves. Its administration favors the many instead of the few; this is why it is called a democracy. If we look to the laws, they afford equal justice to all in their private differences; if no social standing, advancement in public life falls to reputation for capacity, class considerations not being allowed to interfere with merit; nor again does poverty bar the way, if a man is able to serve the state, he is not hindered by the obscurity of his condition. The freedom, which we enjoy in our government, extends also to our ordinary life. There, far from exercising a jealous surveillance over each other, we do not feel called upon to be angry with our neighbor for doing what he likes, or even to indulge in those injurious looks, which cannot fail to be offensive, although they inflict no positive penalty. But all this ease in our private relations does not make us lawless as citizens. Against this fear is our chief safeguard, teaching us to obey the magistrates and the laws, particularly such as regard the protection of the injured, whether they are actually on the statute book, or belong to that code which, although unwritten, yet cannot be broken without acknowledged disgrace".[38]

---

38 Thucydides, *The History of the Peloponnesian War*, trans. Richard Crawley, II, pp. 37–8: 3 May 2018 http://www.gutenberg.org/files/7142/7142-h/7142-h. htm#link2H_4_0007.

Clashes between Democracy, Despotism, and Totalitarianism

The values expressed in the Greek system of Democracy, clashed significantly with the political system of Despotism of Persia, and the political
system of Totalitarianism of Sparta. Back in time, what it meant to be Greek
was imbedded in controversy. What it means to be European in today's
world is also imbedded with inherent controversy. The controversies experienced today may be traced back to Europe's historical roots.

Three central countries of Europe illustrate conflicting political ideologies
of ancient times: Central Greece, Persia and Sparta. The Persian Empire,
between the the mid seventh century B.C and the years 550 B.C. and., was
comprised of a series of dynasties, and an empire ruled by a succession of
rulers or leaders. All these leaders were from the same family or line of
decent.

Persia was then centered in modern day Iran. When Alexander the Great
conquered Persia, Persia covered much of the Ancient world. Sparta was
another powerful country. Sparta was located next to Athens. Sparta was
most powerful when it defeated Athens in the Peloponnesian War (431
B.C. to 404 B.C.). Spartan men were professional soldiers, and values were
reflected in the political structure, which emphasized duty, discipline and
endurance. Spartan dominance was short lived in history.

Opposing political systems created much conflict in the ancient world,
and ideological conflict continues into our present world. Democracy,
totalitarianism, and despotism were three examples of opposing political
systems. Greece embraced a system of democracy, Sparta embraced totalitarianism (the state having complete control and authority), and the Persian
political system was despotic (one ruler having complete authority).

The first known democracy originated in the Greek city – state[39] of
Athens, in about the fifth century B.C. Power was exercised directly through
the elected government. Only Athenian men over the age of twenty-one,
whose parents were both citizens, could be elected.

Democracy was a unique achievement of the Greek culture. Democracy
continues to be a characteristic feature of European and Western culture.
Western people today still understand and value a democratic worldview.

---

39 A Greek city state was known as a Polis.

Different forms of democracy have survived for over two and a half thousand years.

Democracy consisted of the following elements: free and fair elections, active participation by citizens, and a rule of law which stated that all laws and procedures applied equally to all citizens. Athens was the first country to embrace the concept about individuals having inherent value. During this time period, there were three classes of people living in Greece. These three classes included the free citizens of Athenian origin; the Metoik people, who were usually foreigners but not slaves; and lastly, the slaves. The Metoik people and the slaves were both exempt from holding political office. In ancient Greece, the Metoik[40] people were foreign residents of Athens.

Slavery was common in many societies during this era, including ancient Greece. In Greece, most activities were open to slaves except politics, which was reserved for citizens. One of the largest slave populations in the region was centered in Athens. Slaves were required to work in the fields of agriculture, mining, and as domestic servants.

With the advent of democracy, a new method of achieving power came into being. Now power was achieved through verbal persuasion, rhetoric, and sophistry. An expert in rhetoric is someone whose words are used to impress, persuade, inform, and motivate audiences, possibly using words that are elaborate and exaggerated. Originally, Sophists were Greek teachers of rhetoric and philosophy, and were prominent in the fifth century B.C. The Greek term originally referred to a person who is wise or an expert. Isocrates (436 B.C.–338 B.C.) was one of the most influential Greek rhetoricians of his time. He made many contributions to rhetoric and education, through his teaching and written works. He was known for his sensitivity to morality. Some considered him to be one of the original sophists. The term sophist has many negative connotations. Sophistry is a form of reasoning that is not plausible, yet it seems to be credible on a superficial level. It implies having the intent to deceive.

Plato (427 B.C.–347 B.C.) was a Greek philosopher who was considered to be one of the greatest minds to have ever existed. He is one of the three

---

40 The word "Metoik" derives from *metic*, Greek *métoikos*: from *metá*, indicating change; and *oîkos*, indicating dwelling.

fathers of western philosophy, along with Socrates and Aristotle. Plato was one philosopher who described sophists in negative terms. He postulated that sophists were deceivers who were primarily motivated by money, and who were willing to say anything to win an argument. The general negative image of the sophists may be exaggerated.

Despotism, the form of government of Persia, was a form of government in which one person ruled with absolute power and authority. The word "despot" derives from the Greek word *despotes* and means master, or the one who has the power. Local chieftains, simple rulers, kings and emperors exercised this power. Despotism denotes the absolute authority and power as held by the Pharaohs of Ancient Egypt, the nobility in Byzantine courts, and the Byzantine emperors.[41]

Mussolini coined the term totalitarianism in the early 1900's. Mussolini was an Italian politician, journalist, and leader of the National Fascist party from 1922 to 1943. Mussolini eliminated democracy and set up a legal dictatorship.

Totalitarianism is a political system in which the state has complete control and authority over all aspects of the people, both private and public. Everything is politicized, both spiritual and human. Sparta exercised totalitarianism. Sparta subjugated all people to the state, leaving no room for the rights of the individual's public or private life. Worship of the state, statolatry, was required. Despotism and totalitarianism have one key difference. In a system of despotism, one person is the ruler. In totalitarianism, everything is for the state and everything is the state.

Over the course of time, there were multiple confrontations and clashes between the Greeks, the Persians, the Asians, and those from the orient.

---

41 However, the difference between totalitarianism, tyranny, and despotism, should be kept in mind. Totalitarianism is a modern form of statolatry, i.e. the state is organized into a form of government in which the state is the ultimate aim. Tyranny is the reign of an entity, which has absolute power, but it is transferred by the people. Despotism is also the reign of an individual, but the source of this power has a religious character, and it involves the theological identification of the ruler with a deity. In the latter case, the prototype of despotism can be found not in Persia, but in ancient Egypt. In reference to the despotism of Persia, see Richard N. Frye, *La herencia de Persia* (Madrid: Ediciones Guadarrama,1965), p. 127.

The Greek people considered the Persians and the Asians to be enemies of Greek values.

When reading the dramatic writings of the playwright Aeschylus (523 B.C.–456 B.C.), one could become captivated by his tragic stories. In his play entitled "The Persians", Aeschylus gave artistic expression to Persian characteristics. He portrayed the Persian people as having unbridled sensuality, insatiable cruelty, a love and need for luxury, and pride.[42] Aeschylus fought in two wars, first in the battle of Marathon[43], later in the battle of Salamis.[44] It may be postulated that he wrote about tragedy because of his personal war experiences.

Authors such as Hippocrates, Aristotle and Pericles, wrote about the unique Greek culture. They did not make a connection between the values of Greece, and with Europeanism. Others, such as the rhetorician philosophers, did make the connection between Europeanism and Greek values. The presence of rhetoricians was crucial for the developing democracy. Rhetoricians expressed opinions that influenced the evolution of democratic thought and practice.

In any book about a history of philosophy that involves the Greek culture and its Europeanness, misconceptions about rhetoricians abound. Rhetoricians are accused of relativism (a belief in which there is no absolute truth), and subjectivism, (a belief that there is no external or objective truth).[45]

These misconceptions are well-known opinions in the western world. Misconceptions sometimes keep people from being able to recognize the

42 Manuel García Sánchez, *El gran rey de Persia. Formas de representación de la alteridad persa en el imaginario griego* (Barcelona: Universidad de Barcelona, 2009), pp. 42–3.
43 The Battle of Marathon took place in 490 BC, during the first Persian invasion of Greece. The battle was fought in hopes subjugating Greece. The Greek army defeated the more numerous Persians, marking a turning point in the Greco-Persian Wars. https://www.britannica.com.
44 The Battle of Salamis took place in 480 B.C., and was a naval battle fought between an alliance of Greek city-states and the Persian Empire. The outnumbered Greeks were victorious. https://www.britannica.com.
45 Werner Jaeger, *Paideia. The Ideals of Greek Culture*, vol. 1, (Oxford: Basil Blackwell, 1946), pp. 286–331.

truth as delivered from the messenger. The first philosophers who may have propagated misconceptions about Rhetoricians could have been Socrates, then Plato, and then Aristotle. Rhetoricians continue to this day, to be often misunderstood.

In spite of Rhetoricians being hampered by misconceptions, Rhetoricians strongly contributed to the organization of attributes and characteristics (classifications) of Greek values. They were the ones who made the connection between the Greek values of democracy, and Europeanism. They openly spoke against values that were represented primarily by Asia.

Pan Hellenism and Culture

Greek Philosophers were influential in the development of a universal and common culture. The attributes defining culture included: the thought processes of the people, religion, language, and the right for all people to experience personal freedom and universal education. The word "pan" is used in the Greek language to signify all, and Hellen signified Greece. Hellenization referred to: firstly, the implementation of a universal Greek culture over the foreign peoples whom the Greeks conquered, and secondly, to those who wanted to share the Greek culture with the Greeks. Because of this universal value of the Greek culture, everything could be Hellenized.

During the time period between the eight century B.C. and the fourth century B.C., Europe still encompassed only Greece. Up until this time in history, some prominent philosophers and authors, including Hesiod, Herodotus, Plato, Aristotle, Aeschylus, Euripides, and Xenophon, ascribed the title "Europe" to be either a mythological name, or, the name of a continent.

At the same time in history, changes were emerging in the cultural development of Europe. Some of these modifications arose because of famous philosophers of the day, whose impact upon culture continues into our present age. What it meant to be European became clearly portrayed though the writings and speeches of these philosophers. The attic orators, or speechwriters, of Ancient Greece, provided such elaborate and popular speeches, that they were influential in shaping Greek culture. Eminent Greeks who were rhetors (orators, teachers of rhetoric and speech) exerted an impact on the elite of their country. Influential Greek culture, and geographical Europe, were not one and the same.

Two of the ten most prominent speakers of the times who did shape the formation and understanding of Greek and European culture, were Isocrates (436–338 B.C.), a rhetorician and teacher, and Lysias (445 B.C.– 380 B.C.), a professional speechwriter. Isocrates and Lysias were the two philosophers who provided new meaning to the words culture and freedom. Isocrates defined culture, and Lysias defined freedom.[46] The writings from Isocrates provide important historical information about the intellectual and political life of Athens. Lysias, because of his unpretentious simplicity, became a model for plain speech.

Both Isocrates and Lysias provided crucial meaning to Europe in terms of its civilization, a word that was not invented until the end of the eighteenth century. Isocrates and Lysias were so influential in the development of Greek culture and thought, that due attention will be given to their writings.

Isocrates, Culture and Thought

Isocrates was best known for his influence upon culture and Hellenistic thought. Isocrates was one of the ten Attic orators (influential public speakers), and was one of the most persuasive rhetoricians of his era. Through his teaching and literary achievements, he made significant contributions to rhetoric and education.

---

46 This love of freedom manifested itself in very specific situations which sometimes required great courage. In the case of the Greek person, the mentality (the way of being) of a free person emerged and it did not waver even in the face of death. Freedom was not characteristic of subjects in a despotic system. A Roman historian cited the conversation between Darius, a Persian, with Charidemus, a Greek. Charidemus, told the historical story about a king who ordered the execution of a person who provided him with advice that angered him. Then the Greek, remembering his free birth, said: "I have at hand an avenger of my death; that very man against whom I have warned you will exact punishment for the scorning of my advice." Charidemus retained the characteristics of a free man until his death, a luxury and benefit only given to a free Greek man. Quintus Curtius, *History of Alexander*, trans. John C. Rolfe (Cambridge: Harvard University Press, 2006), III, ii, 18.

Isocrates identified the Trojan War as being a turning point in the history of Europe. This war separated and defined differences between Greek Europe from Troy. The people of Troy were considered to be the barbarians of Asia. A legendary conflict between the early Greeks and the people of Troy in Western Anatolia, was depicted through a mythical story, dating back to the twelfth or thirteen century B.C. Some consider the folklore to be a story based upon fact. This legend has inspirited art, philosophy, and stimulated the thinking of generations. It involves Helen, the Queen of Sparta, and Priam, the handsome King of Troy, who lived during the Trojan War.[47]

In the legend, Priam abducted Helen. In response, the Greeks unified and organized a joint war expedition against the barbarians of Troy. The Greek victory was a first for Europe, allowing the Greek people to raise the banner of victory over Asia for the first time.... In the story, Helen's husband Menelaus convinced his brother Agamemnon, king of Mycenae, to lead a rescue expedition to retrieve the abducted Queen. Thousands of ships crossed the Aegean Sea to rescue her and demand her return. A famous Trojan horse, a horse full of soldiers, was left outside the gates of Troy. The Trojans brought this horse into the city, allowing the Greeks entrance to the city, and victory over the Trojans. According to Isocrates, Helen's kidnapping was a blessing. Greece was required to face the more powerful Persia. Due to their overwhelming victory, the Greeks began to see themselves as a culture superior to Persia. They now began to define themselves as being European, and belonging to Europe.

Isocrates contributed Hellenistic thought to Greek culture (pan Hellenism: pan 'all' and Hellas: Greece). He believed that the essence of being European was the universal Hellenism. Hellen, in Greek mythology, was the person from whom all Hellenes (Greeks) were descended. The name Hellen is used with reference to those who are part of common culture rather than from their origin. It was based upon the assimilated culture, and not on ethnicity, race, or nationalism. Isocrates sought to Hellenize geographical Europe; unifying its language and customs. Hellenization has been associated with the adoption of Modern Greek culture and the ethnic

---

47 *Helen* – is the title of a speech given by Isocrates about Helen who was kidnapped and taken to Troy.

and cultural homogenization of Greece. Isocrates wanted the universality of the Greek culture to be open to all who wished to acquire it. As history unfolded, Greece lost its independence when empires changed. Largely due to the influence of Isocrates, Athens remained the capital of world culture, continuing after the Greeks lost their independence.

Isocrates was disturbed about the Persian barbarians in Europe. The word "barbarian" was the word used in reference to those persons who were neither Greek, nor Hellenized. His concern was about the quality of life of the Asians compared with the Macedonians (Greeks). Asia was flourishing and enjoying a greater affluence than the Greeks in the Macedonia of Europe.

To facilitate the cultural Hellenization of the Persian barbarians in Europe, Isocrates influenced the king of Macedonia, King Philip (346 B.C.), the father of Alexander the Great, to intervene in the conflict between Athens and Macedonia. Isocrates claimed that an agreement was required to facilitate unity between the conquered peoples with Greece. In Isocrates's presentation to King Philip, he stated that Greece and Persia differed in their approach to wealth and culture. Isocrates held that Greece highly valued culture, and struggled to maintain a Greek identity. Isocrates believed that Persia remained uncultured and uncivilized (barbarian) in spite of its wealth.

Isocrates' vision of a universal Greek Culture survived the test of time. One reason for this may have been because of his unique perspective about what qualities comprised humanness. Isocrates was one of the first Greeks to stress the qualities that make a person human, which is the capacity for human thought and reason. He described human thought and reason in this way: the mind speaks through the use of a word, the mind and word together are developed and educated by means of philosophy and the Greek specialty, rhetoric.

The following description of philosophy is taken from one of Isocrates' speeches:

> "Philosophy, moreover, which has helped to discover and establish all these institutions, which has educated us for public affairs and made us gentle towards each other, which has distinguished between the misfortunes that are due to ignorance and those which spring from necessity, and taught us to guard against the former and to bear the latter nobly—philosophy, I say, was given to the world by our city. And Athens it is that has honored eloquence, which all men crave and envy in its possessors; for she realized that this is the one endowment of our

nature which singles us out from all living creatures, and that by using this advantage we have risen above them in all other respects as well; she saw that in other activities the fortunes of life are so capricious that in them often the wise fail and the foolish succeed, whereas beautiful and artistic speech is never allotted to ordinary men, but is the work of an intelligent mind and that it is in this respect that those who are accounted wise and ignorant present the strongest contrast; and she knew, furthermore, that whether men have been liberally educated from their earliest years is not to be determined by their courage or their wealth or such advantages, but is made manifest most of all by their speech, and that this has proved itself to be the surest sign of culture in every one of us, and that those who are skilled in speech are not only men of power in their own cities but are also held in honor in other states. And so far has our city distanced the rest of mankind in thought and in speech that her pupils have become the teachers of the rest of the world; and she has brought it about that the name Hellenes suggests no longer a race but an intelligence, and that the title Hellenes is applied rather to those who share our culture than to those who share a common blood."[48]

In the fifth century, the Greeks and the Persians were in conflict. Conflicts between the Greeks and the Persians paralleled earlier wars and conflicts. One conflict transpired between the Greeks against the Thracians, an ancient Indo–European people who inhabited South-Eastern Europe. The second conflict in Greek "memory", were the conflicts between the Greeks against the mythical tribe of female warriors, the Amazons.

Education in Greece during the fifth century became highly valued as a basic human right, due to its inherent nature of promoting freedom. Isocrates founded a school whose goal was to form individuals into people who had a good general knowledge about a variety of subjects. His program of education was called: general education, or liberal arts (hence the Latin *artes liberales*). This program emphasized academic learning. Gymnasiums were established for the purpose of promoting basic physical, and literal education for children and teenagers.[49] Literal

---

48 Isocrates, "Panegyricus," in *Isocrates*, trans. George Norlin (Cambridge; London: Harvard University Press; 1980), pp. 47–50.

49 In present times, sciences available in the educational systems may include physics, chemistry, and mathematics. In the ancient system of education, subjects studied included grammar, rhetoric, and logics (the trivium). Grammar was studied from excerpts taken from the best of poetry and novels. Rhetoric developed a person's ability to create one's own texts from poetry, novels and speeches

refers to the provision of a good education in the most important works of literature.[50]

As knowledge grew, more subjects were later included in educational programs. Subjects' included mathematics (quadrivium), physics, chemistry and others. Education was referred to as academic.[51] Currently, the term gymnasium refers to a secondary school that is focused upon preparing students for advanced academic study in a university.

Subjects to be taught in these Greek schools included Greek values and ideals, as well as the classical subjects of Greek, Philosophy, and rhetoric.

These Greek schools were so efficient in their design that curriculums continued to be used as an educational model in Europe until the second half of the nineteenth century. Gymnasiums designed by Isocrates endured the test of time for over 2000 years. Particular studies, such as Rhetoric,

---

including political ones. And finally, logics developed the ability to be able to think, to speak, and to write in a rational way.. See the following web site : http://www.angelicum.net/degree-program/great-books-program/.

50 *Homo litteratus*: was the term used to refer to a person who received a good education about works from the best poets and writers including Homer, Virgil, Dante, etc. – The educated person would be able to read in both one's own language and in the original language that it was written in. The information learned would contain the best works from authors that belonged to his or her national canon (historical texts one wants to preserve).

51 Interest to reader: It was challenging for the authors to find the correct word to signify the education program developed in ancient Greece. As the two authors debated this challenge, we eventually understood that the word *academic* had a different meaning in the English language when compared with the Polish language. The problem is that many European languages including English and Polish assimilated Greek and Latin words. When the word was assimilated, it was given a different meaning. Both the English and Polish languages ascribe a different meaning to the word *academic*. Another problem that may interest the reader is a problem that can exist between people who speak the same language, but the mother tongue of one may be different. Conflict, misunderstandings and confusion may develop between two people speaking the same language, when one of those persons first spoke a language that ascribed a different meaning to one word. For example: the English word *mentality* has a very different meaning to the French word *mentalité*. When people communicating know only one language, they may understand one word in conversation to have the same meaning. Misunderstandings can occur when these same people first understood a word to have a different meaning in another language.

were compulsory in classical gymnasiums in the Interwar period, the period between the First World War (1914–18) and the Second World War (1939–45) in Poland. Today these studies continue to be compulsory in some countries including Germany and Italy, where such gymnasiums still operate.

In summary, the study of Isocrates provides important historical information about the intellectual and political life of Athens. His contributions include the creation of a universal and well-rounded educational model that is still used in some parts of the world. This model included the provision and availability of education as a right for all, and rhetoric. He provided a definition of those qualities that make a person human (the capacity for thought and reason); he contributed Hellenistic thought, a form of thought that unified language and customs of various parts of the world; and he outlined the differences between Greek Europe and those from other parts of the world. Largely because of Isocrates, Athens remained the capital of Greek (world) culture for many generations.

Lysias and Freedom

Lysias, the second of the aforementioned orators, viewed Europeanism and culture as did Isocrates. Lysias is best known for stressing the notion of freedom, a value held in high esteem during this era.

Persians sought to control and enslave the world. Heroic Greek men fought against Persian domination and tyranny during the Corinthian war, (395–386 B.C.).[52]

One of Lysias's most famous speeches was delivered in honor of the heroic soldiers killed during the Corinthian war. In the following funeral oration, the name Europe was referred to four times:

> "For indeed, being of noble stock and having minds as noble, the ancestors of those who live here achieved many noble and admirable things; but ever memorable and mighty are the trophies that their descendants have everywhere left behind them owing to their valor. For they alone risked their all in defending the whole of Greece against many myriads of the barbarians.

---

52 The Greek conflict of the Corinthian War involved Sparta against the Persian backed coalition of Thebes, Athens, Corinth, and Argos.

The King of Asia was not content with the wealth that he possessed. He wanted to enslave Europe[53] and to dominate the rest of the Greeks.[54] He dispatched an army of five thousand, assuming that he would either obtain the willing friendship of this city or overwhelm its resistance. In another speech in connection with the victorious Battle of Plataea (479 B.C.)[55], Lysias emphasized the importance of freedom. He said: "On that day they brought the ventures of the past to a most glorious consummation; for they secured a permanence of freedom for Europe[56]

Lysias's speech described the Greek people to be courageous and noble, and to be a people undaunted by the superior forces of the enemy who sought to enslave them.

In summary, Lysias became a model for plain speech. He provided meaning to Europe and its civilization. He provided a concept of freedom, not previously thought of in those terms. In his funeral speech, he described the Greek people as curious and noble, with a strong determination to resist enslavement.

Science, Theory, Truth, and Culture

Culture is integral to the unity of a people, and facilitates the development of personality. The Greeks began to characterize the European culture through a variety of themes. Greek culture became further defined and developed through specified fields of study, including: science, theory and truth; morality and good behavior (Praxis); productivity and beauty (Poiesis); religion; mythology; laws; human freedom and human rights; human value and dignity; and later Christianity.

The civilizations of both Egypt and Babylon are more ancient than was the civilization of Greece. Each civilization made contributions to the developing understanding of science. Although astronomy was missing in

---

53 The Greek expression for enslaving Europe is "Europen doulosesthai".

54 *Lysias*, trans. Walter R.M. Lamb (Cambridge: Harvard University Press; London: William Heinemann Ltd., 1930), pp. 20–1.

55 Winning the battle of Plataea was a huge victory for the Greeks and Greek allies against the Persian Empire of Xerxes.

56 *Lysias*, 47. The Greek expression "eleutherian tei Europei" was used to denote "freedom for Europe", or to free Europe.

ancient Babylonia in the strict sense of the word, the Babylonian civilization explored the stars. Astrology was studied in order to predict the future of the king, kingdom, or the people.

The Egyptian civilization developed rudimentary metrology, the scientific study of measurement. Egyptians were interested in both tax collection and the construction of pyramids. Measurement was required for both of these endeavors. Plots of land, which had been flooded by the Nile, needed to be measured in order to collect appropriate taxes. Calculations were required in order to construct pyramids.

The achievements of the Babylonians and Egyptians were often astounding when considered by today's standards. Knowledge had not yet developed into a science, geometry was still unknown, and skills were developing slowly.[57]

The Greeks provided new insights into the development of scientific theory and truth, which in turn provides an understanding of culture and cultural development.

In Greece, the study of science in a strict sense of the word appeared. Science became an open and rational search for truth, aiming to discover truth in a methodical and justified way. Science was not simply a practical skill, or a secret initiation. The search for truth through the sciences became significant in a culture having its roots in Greece. The search for scientific truth may be considered as the beginning, the first significant trait of the so – called European culture.

The Greeks were the first to study cognition, the mental action, or the process, of acquiring knowledge and understanding, through thought, experience, and the senses. The value of cognition, in itself, was first approached philosophically. Later, the study of thought was evaluated as a means to explore culture through other sciences. Other earlier cultures studied cognition in order to rule, learn, or to collect taxes. The study of cognition was now evolving; its aim was to learn about truth for its own sake, and to observe reality with love and understanding. Once science became a study onto itself, a rapid growth of clearly diversified sciences followed.

---

57 John Burnet, *Early Greek Philosophy* (London: Methuen and Co.,1930), pp. 1–30.

New scientific studies were divided into their own bodies of systemized knowledge. The new sciences that began to be studied included philosophy, natural sciences, mathematics and auxiliary sciences like logic and methodology. The Greek culture now reached a knowledge base that allowed for the study of a variety of sciences to blossom.

Morality, Behavior, and Culture

Aristotle was the first to profoundly study ethics, economics, and politics. Human behavior became a new area of interest to be studied by the Greeks in their pursuit of knowledge. The study of human behavior was more suited to a practical application of knowledge (the field of praxis), versus the application of scientific theory. Today, this principle of practical research would be termed qualitative, verses quantitative research.

The Greeks began to develop an interest in studying, examining, and adhering to values. The values (goals) were obtained through the virtues (the means to obtain them). For instance, the value of ethics may be achieved through the virtues of fairness and respect; the value of justice may be achieved through the virtues of fairness and integrity.

Principles were applied in order to move society towards the human good, family and country. Following Homer, who was known for his poetry, the Greeks began to link human activities with education. The development and improvement in the knowledge and practice of human virtue was enhanced though education.

People began to have awareness, and a desire for the good. When one focused upon the good, proper conduct followed. People began to aspire to living a life of virtue. To live by good moral standards, an examination of personal behavior was required. Good human conduct was highly valued. Kalokagathía was a word used by classical Greek writers to describe the personal conduct of a gentleman, especially in a moral sense. Good human conduct became the ideal of moral education. A socialized and civilized society was beginning to develop.

Universal education became highly valued as a right. Education was to be made available to all, and not restricted to the Greek people or the aristocracy. Universal education was believed to promote the good of individuals and the common good of society.

Ethics and ethical principles were studied and evaluated to determine any right course of action in any given situation. The study of ethics was associated with human good, and was applied in all spheres of human endeavors. Political decisions, the economy and economic development, were all linked with the good of individuals, the family, the community, and society. Today, the study of ethics continues to be required in many current educational curriculums, including health care and education.

Aberrations occurring in society, were analyzed, to determine why those unwelcome departures from what is considered to be normal, usual, or expected, had occurred. Defects of society would be examined using the study of ethics and ethical principles. For instance, infidelity and the impermanence of marriage would be examined economically. Degenerate regimes, (including tyranny or oligarchy), and democracy, would be examined politically.

A number of issues, including the acceptance of slavery, were still discursive (requiring discussion); their limitations could be overcome exactly due to their discursiveness. A philosophical method would be used to divide complex issues into smaller and simpler categories.

Analytical reasoning was the method used to resolve difficult and complex problems. Large issues were broken down into simpler or more basic segments, to be examined unit by unit. Then, a conclusion could be reached because of reason and not intuition. When the sciences of anthropology were combined with sociological and historical perspectives, the truth about the human could be examined. Owing to the Greeks, morality took on a both a universal and a human dimension.

Productivity, Beauty, and Culture

Greek culture became further defined through an appreciation of beauty, mythology, and later through Christianity. The political system of Democracy began. Laws stemming from democracy were developed based upon a fundamental value of freedom. As human thought began to evolve, an appreciation of art, beauty, philosophy, morality, human freedom, human rights, and law, also began to evolve.

In this stage of philosophical thought and development, Greeks focused on reason, how men and women derive meaning, and the human ability to notice and reproduce beauty. The world, in which people created and lived, was neither animal nor superhuman. Using human reason, the person was able to derive meaning from the universe. Human reason was used to notice the natural beauty, harmony and order of the universe. The Greeks began appreciate beauty. The ability to reason was used to direct human production. Words such as logos, pathos, and ethos found their way into language. Logos referred to the facts and evidence of an argument, pathos was the appeal to emotion, and ethos referred to the ethics and credibility of the person making the argument.

Through the ability to reason, individuals could rationally form expression to observed beauty and produce something in order to express the beauty they witnessed and experienced.

A special relationship was found between the beauty of the ordered universe, with the beauty of conduct, and the beauty of art. Products made were meant to give artistic expression to the beauty (*poiesis*) of the world and universe in which people could see and live in. In philosophy, the ancient Greek word *poiesis* was derived from an ancient Greek term, which means, to make. The word *poiesis* is used to denote the activity in which a person brings something into being that did not exist before. In the eighteenth century, "fine arts" was the term used to describe beautiful products. The study of fine arts is still found in modern day university curriculums.

Religion and Culture

The early Greeks did not have one religion with a clearly defined dogma (a set of beliefs or principles through a central authority), that was determined by a selected priestly caste. The priestly castes were the authorities, especially in nomadic and tribal societies, who lead sacrifices and other religious pagan activities. Later, Christianity occupied Greek thought and practice.

Greek religion was not universal, but was based upon mythology and tradition. Religion was easily affected and changeable based upon three key factors. These factors included the political systems of the region; the place whereby the Greeks created colonies; and the religion of the peoples who invaded the Greek territories. The Greeks easily accepted varying religious traditions. Religion did not constitute any obstacle for the development of culture. In time, the Christian religion became significant in the development of European culture in Europe.

Ancient Greece's worship was Polytheism. Polytheism was a worship based upon the belief in multiple deities. These deities were assembled into a pantheon of gods and goddesses, each having their own religions and rituals. In a polytheistic system such as the system that was in place in ancient Greece, there was a tendency for one divinity, usually male, to achieve the status of king of the gods. Shifts in power structures and social systems would cause the previous king of the gods to be displaced by a new divinity, who would assume the displaced god's attributes and functions. Frequently the king of the gods would have at least one wife, who would be considered to be the queen of the gods.

The Romans considered their god king to be Zeus – Jupiter. The Egyptians considered their god king to be Zeus – Osiris. Zeus – Jupiter was the god of thunder, light, and the sky. He was considered to be protector of the state and laws and was thought of as father. Zeus – Osiris was presumed to have been the god – king who gave Egypt civilization. He was the god of the dead and vegetation. Because Zeus-Osiris was thought to have lived an earthly life, died, and then experienced an afterlife, he was considered to be king of the resurrection.

Christianity was introduced in Greece by among others, a person by the name of Paul of Tarsus. When Paul noticed that the Greeks worshipped an unnamed God, he explained that Jesus Christ was this unnamed God. He taught that Christianity had the status of being a revealed religion by God himself.[58] Christianity began to have a strong influence and impact upon Greek culture and upon Europe as a whole.

---

58 22 "Then Paul stood in front of the Areopagus and said, 'Athenians, I see how extremely religious you are in every way. 23 For as I went through the city and looked carefully at the objects of your worship, I found among them an altar with the inscription, "To an unknown god." What therefore you worship as unknown, this I proclaim to you. 24 The God who made the world and everything in it, he who is Lord of heaven and earth, does not live in shrines made by human hands, 25 nor is he served by human hands, as though he needed anything, since he himself gives to all mortal's life and breath and all things. 26 From one ancestor[he made all nations to inhabit the whole earth, and he allotted the times of their existence and the boundaries of the places where they would

Christianity, while assimilating the Greek culture, relied upon the super-natural revelation of God. Simultaneously, the Greeks valued freedom of discourse conducted between different philosophical schools. The Greeks were open to cultural development that could emerge from further research and development. In perspective, Greek religion was not strongly tied to any one faith. It was easily changeable and adaptable, allowing Christianity to develop. Christianity valued the dignity of people, because they believed that all people belonged to one true God, a God who loved all of his creation.

Additionally, for Christians, Greek philosophy provided a rich foundation for the continued study about the divine (theology), and a defense against aggressive claims to undermine Christian beliefs (polemics). Christianity supported the Greek values of the day, which included freedom; the respect for human dignity; education; and beauty.

Mythology and Culture

Greek mythology was rich. It permanently inspired art, philosophy, morality, and debates about the Earths creation. Greek mythology later became the heritage of the European culture.

Greek mythology influenced the creative arts. The most spectacular impact of Greek mythology was through the medium of art. European painting, sculpture, theatre, literature, and music, are best understood and appreciated through the knowledge of Greek mythology.

Thales of Mellitus (624–546 B.C.) was considered by Aristotle to be one of the first philosophers in traditional Greece, and is recognized as being the first person in Western civilization who engaged in scientific philosophy.

---

live, [27] so that they would search for God[j]and perhaps grope for him and find him—though indeed he is not far from each one of us. [28] For "In him we live and move and have our being"; as even some of your own poets have said, "For we too are his offspring." Acts 17: 22–28: *the New Revised Standard Version Bible, Catholic Edition (NRSVCE),* copyright © 1989, 1993 the Division of Christian Education of the National Council of the Churches of Christ in the United States of America. Used by permission. All rights reserved: https://www.biblegateway.com/theNewRevisedStandardVersionBible/CatholicEdition (RESVCE).

Thales was regarded as the first philosopher who postulated that everything was created from water.[59] Thales's thinking changed the myth about the world looming out of the Ocean.

Freedom and Culture

In the moral domain, Greek mythology respected unbiased law, justice, and ethics. Greek attributes were not to be favored because they were Greek. This attitude played a crucial role in constituting the universal dimension of Hellenism, which will become the heritage of the West.

A fundamental value of freedom influenced the laws and the continued development of democracy. Freedom was central to the Greek concept of Europeanism: personal, cultural, and political. To be free also meant sovereignty from other nations. Personal liberty allowed the individual the freedom to pursue happiness, and to make personal decisions that were not impeded by political systems or by those in power.

The Persians, who aimed to conquer Greece, posed a great threat to the people of Greece. Greek culture required an atmosphere of freedom to flourish. The Persians aimed to deprive Greece of its independence, impose despotism, (cruel, oppressive, absolute power), and consequently destroy what Greece was striving to become.

Historically, in terms of democracy, the recognition of personal liberty was a great discovery. Currently, those who enjoy living in democratic cultures owe much to the development of democracy and freedom as established though the Greek culture.

Law and Culture

The Greeks may be credited as laying the foundation for a culture of law, which became the heritage of Europe and the world. The Greeks and their human centered civilization, was further developed through the Roman Empire, and through Christianity.

Law in many ancient civilizations was under the domain of power, either religious or political. Despotic states classified all people as objects. Objects

---

59 Aristotle, *Metaphysics*, trans. William D. Ross (Oxford: Clarendon, 1928), I, 983b20–984a4: 3 May 2018 http://classics.mit.edu/Aristotle/metaphysics.html.

did not have legal protection. The ruler, not being an object, did have legal protection.

In Greece, people were considered to be subjects and not objects. Greek law considered individual rights and freedoms as an inherent right, belonging to the citizen as a human being. Laws were developed that were based upon values. These values included justice, individual rights, personal freedoms; and interpersonal, social, and religious relationships. Morality was the most distinctive feature. A ruler, under the influence of power, was not permitted to dictate laws, which conflicted with the law as revealed from God. Sophocles' "*Antigone*", was a famous play portraying moral issues and dilemmas as experienced in the conflict between Creon (a villain), and Antigone, a hero.[60]

Although the Romans did not regard their empire as Europe, their contribution to shaping the European Europe, and the Western culture, was enormous. The Romans further developed and organized the entire field of law, which served to maintain and perfect the Greek cultural heritage. With the advent of Christianity and Christian ideals, the development and implementation of law in the Roman world continued. Roman law was implemented in the Western world as the basis of law. Although philosophy, and ideology stemming from other civilizations, impacted the development of law, Roman law has been preserved to this day.[61]

As time progressed, laws were developed that contained a religious and moral dimension. Justice was shaped in order to reach the deepest recesses of the human heart and conscience.[62] Laws were to be understood by virtue of human reason. Roman philosophical thought began to define

---

60 https://www.amazon.com/Antigone-Greek-Tragedy-New-Translations/dp/0195143736.

61 "Almost all contemporary systems of civil law are rooted in Roman law. Within Roman law, a legal terminology was developed with regard to its systematics, concepts and the specific wording used. Contemporary law linked various legal systems, even the ones developed in different social and economics structures. Therefore, Roman law which began in the middle ages, continues to provide a universal language in the legal community. " Władysław Rozwadowski, *Prawo rzymskie. Zarys wykładu wraz z wyborem źródeł (Roman Law),* (Warszawa: Wydawnictwo Naukowe PWN, 1991), p. 21.

62 Jaeger, *Paidei,* chapters IV and VI.

the concepts of eternal and natural law. Eternal law is a law that is based upon an all knowing, eternal God, who is superior to human beings. This God creates from his ideas, as eternal law.

Natural law in the Christian tradition was based upon the eternal law. Natural law, for Christians, develops because of the one supreme God, who implants inclinations in the human person. These inclinations are to live, to recreate in the next generation, and to know and spread the truth. These inclinations have to be ruled by our practical reason in view of the good. Natural law embodied unchanging moral principles that were regarded as a basis for all human conduct. Certain rights belong to humans. These rights are inherent by virtue of human nature. The single God gives these rights to his human created beings. Laws derive from human inclinations, but these inclinations derive from eternal and then natural law.

III. Religion Influences Culture

Religion begins to shape the European culture, having a profound influence upon it. The influence of religion upon Europe's culture will be explored. Clashes and differing belief systems will transpire between Muslims (Islam) and Christians; then divisions will occur within Christianity itself. An anti-Greek (De Hellenization) and an anti-Christianity movement begins. These all create a colorful tapestry of diverging philosophical debates and cultural clashes.

Christianity Offers Culture a Living Style

Christianity and the Greco – Roman culture, formed a unique culture that became the defining characteristic of Europe. It is impossible to discourse medieval philosophy and culture, without discussing the religious impact of Christianity, and then the impact of Islam.

Because Christianity was a key determinant in the formation of a European culture, it is fitting to give an account about the origins of Christianity, what Christians do believe, and how these beliefs have translated into action. Christian beliefs will be contrasted with Muslim beliefs, because the faith of Islam has been, and continues to be one strong apposing factor in Christian Europeanism. This topic will be mentioned in this chapter, and expanded in the following chapters.[63]

---

63 Christians believe in a supreme God who is Love. This God loves unconditionally, and forgives anything and everything if asked. Reconciliation with this God, and with each other, is a mandatory part of being a Christian. For this reason, the God who Christians venerate, is thought by Christians to give people and the world a reason for hope and peace. Bible: see Jeremiah 31:3; 1 john 4:8; 1 john 1:9; Luke 17:4.
The basic premises of the Christian faith are: Jesus Christ of Nazareth was born from a young woman, the Virgin Mary, and was crucified, in Jerusalem, about 2000 years ago. This occurred because some Jewish leaders wanted to have Christ crucified. These Jewish leaders appealed to the Roman leaders who had authority, and these Roman leaders gave Roman soldiers the instruction to crucify Christ. (Acts 2: 32-39)

Christianity was born in the area of the Roman Empire. The Greeks did not have a well-defined religion prior to Christianity. They believed in many gods. St. Paul, when evangelizing the Greeks, found an unnamed god to be part of their belief system. He introduced Jesus Christ, the God incarnate, as being that unnamed god. Eventually Christian theology became the accepted religion in Greece. Christians believe that Jesus Christ was the long-awaited Messiah, the Son of God, as prophesized in the Old Testament to the Hebrews. The Christian religion has thus been termed revealed. Christians thought of and referred to their God as a God who loves, a God who has a triune relationship with his creatures. They think of this God as three persons in one: God as father, God as Son, and God as Holy Spirit.

Initially, Christianity was regarded as one of the Jewish sects of Judaism, the religion having primarily a local character. In only one generation it spread from Syria across Asia Minor and Greece to Rome.[64] The Roman Empire divided into Eastern and western parts, and eventually fell, allowing the religion of Christianity to became more prevalent. Christianity allowed

---

Three facts are widely accepted by scholars: there was an empty tomb, many eyewitnesses testify to having seen Jesus Christ alive after this crucifixion, and there was a sudden rise in Christianity following these events.

Christians believe five key concepts: These include: God the loving and intimate father created human beings to be in relationship with him; the relationship he created his creatures to have with him was broken by sin (personal choices that distance people from God, choices that began with Adam and Eve); a person by the name of Jesus Christ of Nazareth restored humanity's relationship with the father through his death on a cross, and resurrection back to life; Jesus offers each individual a choice to accept or reject the relationship that God offers; the means to accept this offer of forgiveness is through a personal belief in and accepting Jesus, and through believing in the gospel (the holy bible). Many protestants believe that through the acceptance of Jesus and reciting an acceptance prayer, they are "saved". Catholics include other necessary aspects in developing right relationship with God, and include receiving the sacraments. The sacraments include baptism, confirmation, repentance and seeking forgiveness for sin, and attending mass and receiving the eucharist on a regular basis. Catholics also believe that a person's life choices, and not just acceptance of Jesus, is necessary. Christians believe that Jesus is "living", and it is possible and important to have an intimate relationship with him through prayer.

64 Dawson, *Europe and the Seven Stages*, p. 138.

for the continuation of the great classical Greek and Roman culture.[65] The period between the fifth and fourth century B.C., was the period of Classical Greece. Greek political democracy; and scientific, mathematic, and artistic developments, formed a foundation of the Western culture.

As a religion, Christianity introduced a new, revealed and universal religion into the classical culture, which, until this time in history, was possessed by neither the Greeks nor the Romans. Christianity was able to adapt and implement the classical Greek culture of the times. The practice of Christianity allowed other fields of culture to be modified or supplemented. These fields implemented the values of theory, practical application, and beauty (*praxis* and *poiesis*).

Christianity developed, deepened, and increased the understanding and significance of the values of truth, the good, and the beautiful. In the field of theory, there was a place for scientific theology. In the domain of praxis (morality) there was room for grace and supernatural virtues. In the domain of poesies (beauty), the place for figurative art was preserved in the Greek culture. Idolatry was something to be resisted by the religion and culture of Judaism. Because the Christians of the time were afraid of falling into idolatry, they resisted the figurative art of the Greeks. Because truth, theory, practical application of knowledge, and beauty, were appreciated, these values were easily implemented by non-Christian societies, giving it a universal and European dimension.

Moving forward in time, Christianity played a crucial role in the constitution and protection of Europeanism. After the fall of the Roman Empire, Christianity inherited and procured the treasure of the Greco–Roman culture. The Greco–Roman culture was unique, and became a defining characteristic of Europe. The Greeks discovered the values of truth, the good, and the beautiful. This culture later constituted Europe, since other parts

---

65 "Prudentius perceived the historical destiny of Rome, to open the way for Christianity as a universal religion. He also underlined the value of Roman culture even more than the Greeks perceived them being Greek: 'Romanism differs from barbarism as a man differs from an animal, and as he that has speech differs from one who is unable to speak, and as Christianity differs from paganism." Dawson, *Making of Europe,* p. 30, footnote 8.

of the world ceased to be Christian or European. A specific moment could be identified, when Christianity did become identified with Europe.

Christianity was significant in the formation of the culture of Europe. Christianity has survived for over 2000 years, in spite of persecution, and torture. Christians experienced much persecution under the Roman Empire (and later throughout history including Communism, and Nazism).[66]

About three hundred years after its inception, Christianity was introduced into the Greek culture, as a means of promoting peace. Charlemagne, the famous king and emperor, united Europe through Christianity, encompassing both its philosophical values and religion. Charlemagne may have chosen Christianity either because of its philosophy, because of its religion, or both. Later, Christianity was the philosophy behind the founding of the European Union. In terms of a philosophy, Christianity offered the qualities of peace and prosperity. For instance, Christians strive to achieve an attitude of love of neighbor, forgiveness, charity, peace, and joy. These translate into behaviors that promote social justice. Concern for the poor, the development and maintenance of hospitals, the founding of universities, and education and scientific research, were developed under Christianity. The most educated and learned of historians were often from the Christian faith. Mother Theresa (1910–1997, founder of Sisters of Charity) used to say: "The fruit of silence is prayer, the fruit of prayer is faith, the fruit of faith is love, the fruit of love is service, and the fruit of service is peace."[67]

---

66 There is a wealth of autobiographies written about people who have been persecuted while remaining true to the Christian faith. Two books of note focus upon this topic. One is a true story of a young German Franciscan monk drafted into Hitler's SS during WWII. The experiences of Goldmann under persecution on account of his faith, form and an inspiring witness to the power of love, faith, and sacrifice. Fr. Gereon Goldmann, *The Shadow of His Wings*, (San Francisco: Ignatius Press, 2000).
The second book is the account of Josyp Jaromyr Terlya, who fought for the cause of Christianity all his life and in the most hostile of circumstances, including the 20 years he spent in prisons and prison camps. Josyp Terelya with Michael H. Brown: *Josyp Terelya. Witness To Apparitions and Persecution in the USSR. An Autobiography* (Milford, Ohio: Queenship Publishing Company, 1991).
67 http://www.vatican.va/roman_curia/congregations/cevang/p_missionary_works/infantia/documents/rc_ic_infantia_doc_20090324_boletin13p14_en.html.

In terms of a religion, Christianity offered the strength to live according to Christian values, only because of a true relationship with one supreme God, who provides this strength. On the exterior it is more natural to keep enemies, to stay angry, and to seek retribution. People look to Christians to form an example of living according to these principles. A poor example of Christian behavior may cause people to turn away and become cynical. Levels of spiritual maturity are multifaceted. Because a person is professed to be Christian, does not guarantee the person actually is one, or knows how to live as one. "The Christian ideal has not been tried and left wanting, it has been left untried."[68]

To live as a Christian involves a lifelong commitment and is not an easy task. Clive S. Lewis (1898–1963) was a Christian author and specialist in Medieval and Renaissance Literature.[69] Some of his quotes attest to the difficulties inherent in living as a Christian: "I didn't go to religion to make me happy. I always knew a bottle of Port would do that. If you want a religion to make you feel really comfortable, I certainly don't recommend Christianity."[70] "No man knows how bad he is until he has tried very hard to be good."[71] "Everyone thinks forgiveness is a lovely idea until he has something to forgive."[72]

Falling short of living up to Christian ideals is common, and requires much soul searching and commitment on a daily basis. People, whether or not they are Christian, may live good lives with integrity. Many postulate that a culture which makes a commitment to live according to Christian values and beliefs is a culture that is more likely to obtain these ideals. Intrapersonal values include love and forgiveness, acceptance and compassion, and recognizing people by their unique gifts of character, versus their shortcomings and failures. Personal goals and values include developing personal character, honesty, developing a joy that comes from living

---

68 Gilbert K. Chesterton, *What's Wrong with the World*, 15.1: 4 May 2018 www.chesterton.org.

69 www.cslewis.com.

70 Clive S. Lewis, *God in the Dock*: 4 May 2018 http://www.notable-quotes.com/l/lewis_c_s.html.

71 Lewis, *Mere Christianity*: 4 May 2018 https://www.goodreads.com/quotes/99392-no-man-knows-how-bad-he-is-till-he-has.

72 Lewis, *Mere Christianity*.

with integrity, being thankful for the blessings that life does offer, offering service to others when needed, valuing of all life, caring for the environment, being willing to begin again after failure, and determination to live in the present moment. During some periods of history, a commitment of peoples to live according to peaceful reconciliation, created a peaceful European community. Whether examined from the standpoint of a religion, or the commitment to live according to a principled philosophy, living in a peaceful manner is paramount for Christians.[73]

Historically, Europe under Christianity provided many benefits to the European culture. It promoted the concept of equality among people, and intellectual growth and progress. It served to unite and bond the people throughout Europe. Equality, freedom and justice, were promoted in the political dimension, emphasizing a freedom that focused upon the common good. Europe under Christianity fostered a care of the poor, the concept of universal education, medical research, and care of the sick.

There exist many misconceptions about the Christian faith and a current, generalized, world prejudice. If examined by the learned, misconceptions about Christianity would prove to be unjust or inaccurate.

---

73 Gilbert K. Chesterton (1834–1936) was a Christian English journalist, art critic, poet, dramatist, philosopher, and theologian, to name only a few of his attributes. Some of his memorable quotes describe Christian thinking well. Some of these include: "To love means loving the unlovable. To forgive means pardoning the unpardonable. Faith means believing the unbelievable. Hope means hoping when everything seems hopeless." "There are two ways to get enough. One is to continue to accumulate more and more. The other is to desire less." "The riddles of God are more satisfying than the solutions of man." "Just going to church doesn't make you a Christian any more than standing in your garage makes you a car." "Education is simply the soul of a society as it passes from one generation to another." "Impartiality is a pompous name for indifference which is an elegant name for ignorance." "Certain new theologians dispute original sin, which is the only part of Christian theology which can really be proved." "As long as you have mystery you have health; when you destroy mystery, you create morbidity." May 2018 www.chesterton.org.

The Christian Faith Attacked

Charles the Great, (Charlemagne, 742–814 A.D.) was the first recognized emperor in Western Europe. Because he united much of Europe, he was called the father of Europe.[74] He supported the Roman (Christian) Church.

In the fourth century, Christianity was widely practiced. Christianity covered a large land mass and included the whole of the Mediterranean Basin.[75] The practice of Christianity had spread over most of three continents, of which the largest part belonged to Africa. In Europe, Christianity still covered a small piece of it, while in other geographical locations; it covered a large area of land. In the Europe of the fourth century, Christianity cannot be identified with Europe.[76]

As time continued throughout history, Christian thinking, philosophies, and values were challenged. In the seventh century, a new religion appeared on the world scene, that of Islam. A Muslim is a person who practices Islam, believing that the word of God (Allah) was spoken to the prophet Muhammad, through the angel Gabriel. This new religion was expansive. Islam chose to honor their faith through the conquering of other nations. Islam quickly conquered at first Asia Minor and North Africa. By the beginning of the eighth century, Islam had conquered Spain.

Historically, Christians have had to defend themselves against Muslim invasions. The Holy Wars, although there were examples of many evils connected with them, were formed with the intention of regaining what was lost for the Christians who lived in territories defeated by Muslim invasions.[77]

The Catholic Church in the middle ages was the collective, and uniting religious institution in Europe. Popes during the middle ages carried much

---

74 The Latin term for Father of Europe is "pater Europae" Charlemagne was given this name because he was able to unify Europe, form a pan European identity, and bring an end to the dark ages.

75 *Mare nostrum*, (Orosius) was a latin word which meant "our sea". The term was used to refer to the Mediterranean Sea.

76 Boer, *Europe*, pp. 21–2.

77 Thomas Madden: "Understanding the Crusades" Dr. Madden discusses myths and misconceptions connected with the crusades. www.lighthousecatholicmedia. org: CD.

political power and influence. This influence was later weakened when conflicts between the church and the state emerged, and then later due to the Protestant reformation. The balance of political powers gradually made Europe the bastion of faith.

Due to Islam invasions, the impact of the Roman (Christian) Church was reduced to a small part of Europe. Europe as a concept took on a symbolic meaning. When the Arabs set out from Spain through the Pyrenees, intending to continue their conquest of Europe, they were defeated by Charles Martel (732 A.D.) in the battle of Poitiers.[78] His army for the first time began to be referred to as European. Charles Martel, (686–741 A.D.) was a military leader, nobleman, and supporter of the Holy See (the Pope). Charles Martel sought to prevent the on-going annexation of Europe by the Arabs.

Another group attacking Western Europe and Christianity were the Hungarian warriors called the Magyars. The Asians (Hungarians) wanted to subdue Europe. Otto the First defeated them in the famous Battle of Lichfield (955 A.D.), in Germany, gaining him the title of liberator of Europe.[79,80]

Throughout the centuries, various political powers continued to attempt to gain control over Europe, threatening the Christian faith. Popes were aware of the need to defend Western Christianity from these attacks. The total Christianization of Europe and its unification were urgently needed.

---

78 The Christian, Charles Martel, was able to stop the Muslim advance into Western Europe, by winning a famous battle titled: the Battle of Tours, near Poitiers France.

79 Boer, *Europe*, pp. 26–7 (the *liberator Europae) in latin*.

80 Otto defended Europe against Hungarians: the proto-Hungarians were apparently an ethnic blend of Ugric and Turkish peoples living in western Siberia. By the early 5th century A.D. they had migrated southwestward and were roaming over the Khazar Turkish empire, centred near the Caspian Sea. By AD 830, however, they were appearing on the west banks of the Don River and, as a body, consisted of seven tribes, who had been joined by three dissident tribes of Khazars known as Kavars. By the late 9th century the Hungarians had entered their present location, subjugating the resident Slavs and Huns there. Until they were checked a half century later, the Hungarians were the scourge of Europe, raiding as far afield as Bremen, Orléans, and Constantinople (the English word ogre, a corruption of "Hungar," attests to their notoriety). https://www.britannica.com/topic/Hungarian-people.

Pope Urban II[81] wrote that Christianity blossomed in Asia, Africa defended Christianity, but as for Europe "even that part of the world belongs in only a small portion to Christianity."[82]

The Christian church was divided through the protestant reformation. Unification of the Christian faiths (Protestant and Roman Catholic) became possible and motivating in the fifteenth century because of the threat posed by Islam, this time coming from Turkey. Byzantium fell to Islam in 1453 A.D. At the time, Byzantium, (Constantinople), was the capital of the Byzantine Empire. It was one of the most heavily fortified cities of the times. The Turks were able to overpower and gain control of Constantinople. Consequently, Europe became the last bastion of Western Christianity and of world Christianity in general. Pope Pius II[83] (1458–1464) spoke about Europe as a Christian Republic[84], and about our Europe.[85] He was the first to introduce the adjective European.[86,87]

Other clashes and turning points continued throughout history. The loss of Christian ideals and behavior led to the rise of Nazism, Fascism, Socialism, and Communism. Although some initial aims of each of these "isms" may have been praiseworthy, the actual outcome was nothing short of horror.

Christian Europe Invaded by Islam

The process of exploring the predominant religions of Europe, continues. Culture and its development are strongly shaped by its religion, the faith of the people, and later culture is impacted by science. Christianity continues to shape European Culture distinctively. The first concept of Europe involved

---

81 Urban II was head of the Roman Catholic church between 1088–99 A.D. He developed and reformed the church, started the Crusade movement, and strengthened the papacy as a political entity. www.britannica.com

82 Boer, *Europe*, p. 28.

83 **Pius II**, was pope between 1458–1464. He was an author, humanist, and politician. He tried to unite Europe in a crusade against the Turks at a time when the Turks threatened to overrun all of Europe. www.britannica.com

84 Latin: Respublica Christiana.

85 Latin: Europa Nostra.

86 Latin: Europeus.

87 Boer, *Europe*, pp. 26–7.

the clash between the Greeks and the Persians. The second concept concerns Christianity and Islam meeting head on.

Christianity became threatened through clashes with Islam and various political powers that attempted to gain control over Europe. Christianity clashed with Islam regarding theological concepts and theories even though Christianity and Islam share some common beliefs. Religion, culture and civilization were the basis of the clash, not geography or the acquisition of territory. As contrasted with the peaceful philosophy of Christians, Islam had a hostile attitude toward Christians, and attempted to take Europe by force.

Since this second concept of Europeanism involves the clash shaped in the context of multiple confrontations between Christianity and Islam, it is prudent to examine in more detail, the main differences that loom out between them. Not only are the strictly religious differences meaningful. The cultural differences are important in demonstrating the extent to which religion itself generates a culture, or the degree to which the religion may accept or reject the existing type of culture. Europeanism and culture are impacted through clashes of fundamental beliefs between Islam and Christianity. Islam and Christianity persist in meeting head on. Christianity continues to clash with Islam. Christian and Muslim faiths differ, causing numerous clashes throughout history. These clashes continue into the present. The religious differences between Islam and Christianity have a huge impact on the entire culture of a given society, both directly and indirectly. The actual impact noted will vary, depending upon the type of civilization within which the religion finds its field of impact.[88]

---

88 Differences between Islam and Christianity are well documented on the following website.
https://www.rotherham.ec/resources/looking-for-answers/whats-the-difference-between-christianity-and-islam
The Koran is the holy book of reference for the Muslims.
"On the other hand, it cannot be claimed that in the Koran there are no injunctions influencing the organization of communal life. The Koran is full of regulations in the field of hygiene, and contains an exact family and property law, entering into even minor details; it also contains an ethical system. The use of the fine arts is assessed precisely, although in the most part negatively. The Koran touches upon the categories of health, prosperity, beauty, goodness. In the category of Truth, it is little concerned with the supernatural (theology negligible beyond expression!) and with the natural hardly at all—only to the extent that family and property law constitute the whole of jurisprudence. But the Koran's

Christianity and Islam: Origins

Two persons were significant in the founding of the two divergent and original doctrines. Starting with the first basic question: Who founded Christianity, and who founded Islam?

Christianity began with Jesus Christ, who was born in what is now modern-day Israel. He stated that he was the Son of God, and incarnated in order to fulfil the prophesies of the Old Testament of the Bible.

Islam began with Muhammad, born 570 years after Christ, in Saudi Arabia (Mecca at that time). Mohammed claimed to have had a series of visions in the years surrounding 610 A.D. These visions prompted him to start a new religion for the Arabic nations. He saw himself as a prophet, messenger, and teacher. His new religion meant submission, or, submitting to God.

Jesus Christ, the founder of the Christian faith, was a person, born about 2000 years ago in the current Israel, to a young woman, believed by Christians to have been a virgin, prior to her inception by the Holy Spirit. Jesus lived approximately thirty-three years prior to his crucifixion. He selected and worked with twelve apostles for about three years during his ministry. He taught his apostles to continue his mission after his death. He was betrayed by one of these apostles (Judas Iscariot), leading to an illegal trial and torturous death.

Jesus Christ died on a cross for crimes he did not commit, was buried, and rose from the dead about three days after his death. Approximately five hundred people following his death saw him alive, and then eyewitnesses

---

shortcomings from the angle of civilization go deeper. All its injunctions are concerned with family life alone, at most with that of the clan, and it knows only private law. There is no law of government in the Koran, so how could government be based on the Koran? Government is left to the will and pleasure of authority, so that the arbitrary will of the ruler becomes an indispensable part of the law. From this it is one step, and an inevitable one, to the arbitrary will of every official. It also becomes necessary to stretch the Koran to meet the needs of the State. Military service was kept up in the name of the holy war. Taxation came under the duty of alms giving. Obligatory alms for the poor was made a State concern, and later, under Caliph Omar, five kinds of such alms taxes were fixed." Felix Koneczny, *On the Plurality of Civilizations* (London: Polonica Publications 1962), VII, 5: 4 May 2018 http://sci.pam.szczecin.pl/~fasting/files/download/Koneczny/strona.htm.

saw him ascend into the sky approximately forty days after his resurrection. During his ministry he healed the sick, changed the weather, walked on water, raised the dead to life, provided teachings about how to live and love with humility, and provided a concept to people about who the unseen God the Father is. Christians proclaim that Jesus Christ was crucified on a cross in order to take on the sin of the world, which would give each person the possibility of eternity with God in heaven, provided the person accepted Jesus Christ into one's heart. According to Christians, the human person, while living on this earth, must decide whether to accept the mercy of God, or receive his judgement.

The death of Christ on the cross is a historical fact, not a legend. The resurrection of Christ is based on indirect certificates, the credibility of which is subjected to scientific analysis. For reference, the book The Case for Jesus explains this in great historical detail.[89]

Muhammad (570 A.D.–June 632 A.D.) is considered to be a prophet by the Muslim faith, and the person who founded the Islamic faith. At the age of forty, Muhammad reportedly received his first revelation from God through the Angel Gabriel. The revelations in written form are collectively known as the Quran (or Koran). He was probably born in what is currently Saudi Arabia. According to Islamic doctrine, he was God's messenger, sent to confirm the teachings of previous prophets. He died at the age of sixty-three. He is thought to be, by his followers, a perfect example of an honest, just, merciful, compassionate, truthful, and brave person.

Mohammed said he was a prophet for the Muslims, while Jesus Christ, according to Muslims, was a prophet for Christians. Averroes, a philosopher of Islam, supported Islam's acceptance of this premise.

There are similarities between the Christian and Muslim faiths, and the people who practice these faiths. Both can include people who are kind, compassionate, loving, and disciplined. Both believe in one true God (as contrasted with cultures that were polytheistic, or atheistic). Both believe they have descended from the great prophet of the Old Testament, Abraham.

---

89 Pitre Brant, *The Case for Jesus. The Biblical and Historical Evidence for Christ* (New York: Image, 2016).

The name of Abraham was Abram prior to his name change. Both believe Abraham was tested by God to sacrifice his son before God intervened.

Christians and those of the Jewish faith believe Isaac from Abraham's wife Sarah was to be sacrificed. Muslims believe the sacrifice would have been Ishmael, the son of Abraham and the Egyptian slave named Hagar. Christians believe this act of sacrifice was to prefigure the actual death of Jesus Christ upon the cross. Jesus was to be a sacrificial lamb, dying on a cross to take the penalty of sin, for the purpose of saving the human race from death. This unselfish act from Jesus Christ, allowed humans a possibility of entrance into heaven.

Christians and Muslims both practice solitary and communal prayer. Both believe an innocent man, Jesus Christ, was condemned to death due to a betrayal by Judas. Christians believe Jesus died on the cross, some Muslims believe someone else took the place of Jesus on the cross. Both Roman Catholic (and some protestant) Christians and Muslims give reverence to Mary, the mother of Jesus. Both worship in similar manners, and may even sing using hymns that have similar rhythms. Both Muslims and Roman Catholics may use beads as a method of prayer. As religions, both would ask God's assistance to live according to their values (philosophy). Both religions have caring people who are charitable and generous. These qualities are not unique to Christianity or Islam. Others who do not have any faith also may exhibit these and many other good qualities. Most faiths, all religions, have extremists. Both Christians and Muslims share a belief in life after death, and share a concept of a Heaven and a Hell.

Christians refer to a Bible, Muslims refer to the Koran (Quran) as a reference for living within the faith, and use this book as a call to action, and as a method of personal development. Christians believe their Bible is a love story between God and his children. God continues to seek out his children in spite of their wandering away from him. Christians prefer peaceful solutions to differences. The Bible references Jesus as teaching his followers to forgive, look the other way, stop sinning, and, the one who is free of sin would qualify to "throw the first stone".[90]

---

90 When they kept on questioning him, he straightened up and said to them, 'Let anyone among you who is without sin be the first to throw a stone at her.' John 8:7 (RSVCE).

Christianity and Islam: Differences

There are many disparities between the Islamic and Christian faiths. Clashes are due to diverging viewpoints. Both Christians and Muslims accept that a God exists. Within that premise, there are a number of theological issues to resolve. First, perhaps a review of the disciplines referred to in this chapter, are referenced: Theology is the study of the Bible, religious faith, practice and experience. Philosophy, in comparison, studies subjects including reality, existence, and knowledge.

A philosopher has primarily written this work. In studying the development of a culture of Europe, the development of Christianity was a strong determinant in Europe's cultural formation. In discussing key beliefs of the Christian faith, it is best to refer to the writings and teaching of prominent Theologians, such as Thomas Aquinas, especially when there is controversy in religious formation and thought.

In discussing the theology and philosophy behind the two religions, the use of the word "MAN" is required.[91] In these instances, the word "MAN" will be put in quotes and capitalized. A concerted effort has been made to use gender respectful language when at all possible.

In order to clarify further these differences for study, and because Christianity had such an impact upon the development of European culture, it is prudent to further explain Christian theology, rejected by Muslims. The Christian perspective as outlined in this account attempts to discuss what is held in common among the different Christian churches. Disparities in beliefs between different Christian denominations will be outlined in a later section of this book.

Briefly, Islam is a religion that believes in one God. Christians believe in a triune God, one God in three persons: Father, Son, and Holy Spirit.

"And Jesus said, "Father, forgive them; for they know not what they do". Luke 23:34: (RSVCE) She said, "No one, Lord." And Jesus said, "Neither do I condemn you; go, and do not sin again." John 8:11 (RSVCE).

"Then Peter came up and said to him, "Lord, how often shall my brother sin against me, and I forgive him? As many as seven times?" [22] Jesus said to him, "I do not say to you seven times, but seventy times seven." Matthew 18; 21–22: (RSVCE)

91 See *Introduction*.

A Muslim would consider a Christian's use of the familiar words of father, and son, to be blaspheming. Christians believe in a God that wants to be in a loving relationship with his creatures:[92] Christians believe in a God who participates with humans, in the human suffering, by dying on a cross. A Muslim believes that God is a master, and his subjects are his slaves.

Let's review what each believes in more detail. Then let's look at how the Christian faith was explained through a prominent Christian philosopher and theologian: Thomas Aquinas (1225–1274 A.D.). Then we will look at the response to faith through Christianity and Islam.

This chapter discusses complicated theories of faith and belief. Theological differences include the concepts about who and what God is; the "Holy trinity"; beliefs regarding what and who Jesus Christ was and is; what God's Will requires; what it means to be human; how the human person came into being, what is the human relationship between humanity with God and the reason human beings were created, the theory of creation and what "original sin" entails; free will and free choice as an influence upon a person's life; and the response to the need to evangelize. As far as the writers can show or analyze regarding Muslim beliefs, some key controversial subjects are referenced. The Christian teachings are spoken of in detail, and then

---

92 "And they heard the sound of the Lord God walking in the garden in the cool of the day". This passage discusses the early relationship that Adam and Eve had with God, who was walking in the garden calling for them. Genesis 3: 8. *the New Revised Standard Version Bible, Catholic Edition (NRSVCE),* copyright © 1989, 1993 the Division of Christian Education of the National Council of the Churches of Christ in the United States of America. Used by permission. All rights reserved: https://www.biblegateway.com/theNewRevisedStandardVersio nBible/CatholicEdition (RESVCE).
"He who does not love does not know God; for God is love". 1 John 4:8 **(RESVCE).**
"How precious is thy steadfast love, O God! The children of men take refuge in the shadow of thy wings". Psalm 36:72 (RESVCE).
"O **Lord,** God of Israel, there is no God like thee, in heaven or on earth, keeping covenant and showing steadfast love to thy servants who walk before thee with all their heart; Chronicles 6:14 (RESVCE).
"For God so loved the world that he gave his only Son, that whoever believes in him should not perish but have eternal life". John 3:16 (RESVCE).

the Muslim counter arguments are presented to illustrate differences. Next follows a philosophical discussion, which may be difficult to understand, for those who are not philosophy or theology experts. It must be included in this text, and is included for the purpose of reference.

The coauthor of this book is not a philosopher. Even after many writings and additions to this book, she admits that she does not understand much of the following section. Professor Jaroszyński gives encouragement: Regarding the subjects in which philosophy entails, one "should" say "I do not understand". Through the process of not understanding, and the process of struggling, studying, and attempting to understand, becomes a best point of departure to start to understand. One becomes intellectually open for truth in itself.

Conceptualizing God

Among the most essential differences between the Christian and Islamic faiths concerns topics including: conceptualizing of God, the concept of "MAN" (the human person), and how the faith is to be propagated. Christians and Muslims differ in their conceptualizing of who and what God is. The conceptualizing of God is not easy to be explained or to be understood. God in himself is not a concept. It is impossible to conceptualize God. What the human person is able to do, is to conceptualize God in our own way. This conception is poor and imperfect, but, it serves as a means of approaching God in some imperfect fashion. Christians and Muslims differ in their concept of who and what God is. The concept of God is not an easy concept to be explained or to be understood.

Both Christians and Muslims believe that there is only one God who is a supreme being (monotheism), as opposed to the Romans for example who believed in the worship of many gods (polytheism), atheists who believe that God does not exist, or agnostics who believe that the concept of God is unknowable. Christians understand God to be absolutely good, powerful, divine, and loving, and a God who in an analogical and perfect way responds as a father would to his family. Christians believe that humans are given their own will, to make their own free choice, about whether to know and have a relationship with him, and whether to have faith. Islam accepts a God who does not allow human subjectivity, hides the truth from persons, and may compel people to do evil.[93] This may lead the Muslims to want to use coercion as a tool for spreading faith.

In looking at these two perspectives, it is helpful to review the dimensions of philosophical anthropology (the study of humans as humans), sociology (humans within past and present societies), and metaphysics (theory of real being). Both Christians and Muslims believe themselves to be descendants of Abraham, a key figure in the Old Testament of the Bible. Christians believe God exists in the trinity, one God in three persons, father, son and Holy Spirit. It accepts the divinity of Jesus Christ, that he was both God and "MAN" (human person). They believe he was completely God, and completely man, having two natures (divine and human). They accept this fact as a mystery of the Christian faith. Christians believe Christ not only died on the cross, but also rose from the dead. This concept of the resurrection is the critical determinant of the Christian faith. Many over the years in attempting to dispute the Christian faith, research this concept.

Islam rejects all of these concepts, accepting one and only one God. Islam believes Jesus Christ existed, that he was a prophet. Muslims explain the crucifixion differently than do Christians. One explanation offered is that someone else took the place of Jesus on the cross, for instance Judas his betrayer, or a secret twin brother of Jesus.

The concept of God as understood by Christianity is unique. Christianity brought a new concept of God, and a new concept of "MAN" to Europe.

---

93 Benedict XVI said: "The decisive statement in this argument against violent conversion is this: not to act in accordance with reason is contrary to God's nature. The editor, Theodore Khoury, observes: For the emperor, as a Byzantine who was shaped by Greek philosophy, this statement is self-evident. But for Muslim teaching, God is absolutely transcendent. His will is not bound up with any of our categories, even that of rationality. Here Khoury quotes a work of the noted French Islamist R. Arnaldez, who points out that Ibn Hazm went so far as to state that "God is not bound even by his own word, and that nothing would oblige him to reveal the truth to us. Were it God's will, we would even have to participate in idolatry." Benedict XVI, *Faith, Reason and the University. Memories and Reflections*, University of Regensburg 12 Sept, 2006: 4 May 2018 https://w2.vatican.va/content/benedict-xvi/en/speeches/2006/september/documents/hf_ben-xvi_spe_20060912_university-regensburg.html.

God is now understood as one God – but in three persons. This Triune God loves his creatures and wants a personal relationship with them. He is respectful, and patiently waits for his creatures to come to him. In fact, he actively seeks his people, and never gives up in trying to form a relationship with them. He never forces himself upon his creatures. He will always accept a person back into right relationship with him, providing that the person is repentant, and freely chooses to have a relationship with God (choosing his mercy). However, the person who refuses this relationship must accept the consequences of the refusal, that is, God's justice.

The concept of God has shifted over time. Plato described God as being the maker of the universe. A divine craftsman, or, "Demiurge" is able to create a world around us by using eternal matter, according to mathematical ideas. The Christian tradition understands the universe as having been created by a real God, who created the universe from nothing. The concept "demiurge" referred to "God like", not a real and tangible God.[94]

Aristotle and Plotinus's view of God is no longer accepted: Aristotle viewed God as being an unmoved – mover, pure intellect only, and Plotinus described God as being totally transcendent, above Being at all.

The Human Person

Differences in beliefs about who the human person is, stem from beliefs concerning human creation. Christians believe humans came into existence, because of God's creation. "MAN" is a person because of being created in the image and likeness of God. People were created to know, love, and serve God in this world in order to be with him in the next. Each person was created individually, is unique and special, and has one's own idea and relationship with God. Before creation, we are simply non-existent. Our relation to God on the metaphysical (ontic level) is not the effect of our choice. If we are, and are who we are, it is because God wants us to exist. We are nothing, and have nothing to say, before we were created. Once created, we have free choice. This choice entails whether or not we want to receive God's salvation, a life in eternity with God, or a life in eternity in hell.

---

94 The word *"ex nihilo" is used to mean* "from nothing".

Christianity has also brought a new meaning and perspective to the concept of being human. "MAN", in the Christian focus, is viewed primarily as a PERSON, as a being that was created in the image and likeness of God.[95]

The Christian concept of existence, reason for existence, and God, has been further defined within philosophical circles. A being (something that exists), has no sufficient reason for existence in itself. It may, or it may not, exist. If it exists, however, it must have a reason for existence outside itself, or, it could not exist. Existence is a unique aspect of being that one cannot compare to any other aspect. One cannot provide examples for such a concept; one can only understand it intuitively, and catch it in an existential judgment. John exists, Eve exists, a tree exists. Existence cannot be conceptualized; it is an act of concrete being. A concept expresses content, which includes the properties of quality, quantity, and localization. Existence is the most fundamental aspect of being. It cannot be conceptualized, and it cannot be divided into more simple elements.

Taken a step further, a being which is created for a purpose, must be created by a being who also has its own reason for being (purpose) in itself. This being that is creating is called God. This creating is continuous, keeping us in existence. When we exist, this creating keeps us existing all the time. It is a dynamic process. We are not created on any given day, and then the creation stops.

The being that God created becomes the being that just exists, created due to participation in God's power, created for a purpose. God has a will and idea for every being that he created. This reason of existence includes the purpose for which it was created; and it also means the Cause of existence.

Christianity provided a new concept and appreciation of God. An appreciation of who God is goes beyond any capacity of the human being fully to understand. Theologically, God has the ability to assume human nature to be divinized.

Through God incarnating and becoming man, there is a possibility to have human life in Union with God. This also opens up the capacity of humans to understand humanity, in terms of human existence (existentially), as

---

95 Latin; prósopon-persona.

well as the possible purpose for the creation of the human person. Without
reference to a possible reason for human creation, the existence and nature
of the human person are still incomprehensible.

Christianity and Islam differ in their fundamental concept about the
human person: Who and what is "MAN". Christian theology bases the
concept of a person as presented in the Bible, the book used as Christian
reference.

The biblical account of creation maintains God created "MAN" in his
own image and likeness. Image represents a person. Image and likeness are
not synonyms. Image and likeness differ in meaning. An image represents
something that is close to God in likeness. Likeness denotes anything that
has been created by God. Some beings (angels) are also image, and are
closer to God than humans. Humans are created according to the image
of God. Being created as an image of God, or according to the image of
God, leads to the idea of a person. Persons have value and worth because
every person is created individually and is as a unique person.[96] The person
is not created as a whole species. The Christian concept of the essence of
"MAN", laid the foundations of personalism, a belief that recognizes the
inherent value and uniqueness of individuals, who have their own free will
and intellect. It is because of this value and belief in the uniqueness and
specialness of each created being of God that leads Christians into prayer
and peaceful activism, in order to promote and protect life at all stages,
from conception to end of life.

Original Sin

Next is the concept of original sin. Original sin, and the guilt and effects of
this original sin, are disputed between Christians and Islam.

Both Muslims and Christians believe the first human being, Adam,
sinned against God. This is called original sin. They differ in their theology about what followed from this act of disobedience towards God.
Christians (Catholics and many Protestants), believe that this original sin
created an inherited guilt upon the whole human species, which effects all
further generations. Because the first people of the Bible, Adam and Eve,

---

96 Latin: persona.

sinned, all generations would carry the effects of this sin, until a Redeemer, Jesus Christ, took the punishment for sin and restored a relationship with God. Because of the effects of original sin, "MAN", is not consistent in doing good. There is room for evil in human behavior, and, evil may be done consciously. One of the greatest Roman poets, Ovid, an author of the poem "Metamorphoses" expressed this problem: "I see what is better, and approve it, but go after what's worse".[97] Saint Paul discussed how difficult it was for him to do the good that he wanted to, instead doing the opposite which he did not want to do. "[98]

Great philosophical scholars attempted to explain philosophical concepts prior to the advent of Protestantism. Protestantism in itself has many varied beliefs connected with the wide range of protestant churches and doctrine. For ease of discussion, concepts will be explained from Catholic theology. (Some protestants share this same theology). Theologically, Catholicism attempts to explain the real human experiences, and human susceptibility to moral evil viewed from the perspective of the whole human species through the concept of original sin. Islam does not differentiate between guilt from the original sin, and the effects caused because of the original sin.

Muslims view the effects of Adam's first sin and disobedience towards God differently than do Christians. Muslims believe Adam's mistake was minor. They believe all humans are born sinless and pure, free from any guilt or sin, and that no sin is inherited. Muslim's believe that the paradise of God's reward is earned through doing good deeds, and everyone is to be judged according to their actions in this life. The need for a redeemer does

---

97 Latin "Video meliora proboque, deteriora sequor" Ovid, *Metamorphoses*, trans. Stanley Lombardo (Indianapolis/Cambridge: Hackett Publishing Company, Inc 2010) 7, 20: 4 May 2018 https://books.google.pl/books?id=mwMLFWjHpQIC &printsec=frontcover&dq=ovid+metamorphoses&hl=pl&sa=X&ved=0ahUKE wjwoNSEzevaAhWLZVAKHS9AB4QQ6AEIJzAA#v=onepage&q&f=false.

98 "For I do not do the good I want, but the evil I do not want is what I do". *Romans* 7:19. *the New Revised Standard Version Bible, Catholic Edition (NRSVCE),* copyright © 1989, 1993 the Division of Christian Education of the National Council of the Churches of Christ in the United States of America. Used by permission. All rights reserved: https://www.biblegateway.com/theNe wRevisedStandardVersionBible/CatholicEdition (RESVCE).

not exist. Muslims do believe that humans do have a susceptibility to sin. They believe that the only thing that can save a person from Hell is their belief in One God, and by adhering to his commandments.

Christians attribute sin due to Adam and Eve: Due to the disobedience against God from the first parents, Adam and Eve, original sin, entered the world. Because of this sin, humanity had lost right relationship with God. A redeemer in the name of Jesus Christ lived, was born of a woman, and died on a cross in order to remove the guilt of this sin, and restore people to right relationship with God. In the Christian view, the sin committed by the first parents, Adam and Eve, became the heritage of humankind. All generations were affected by this sin, causing the human race to easily do things, to sin, that would continue to cause separation from God. Christ suffered and died in order to take the penalty, and heal the separation, caused from sin. People, through free will, may accept or reject God, and reject having a life with him in eternity. The gift of free will is an important concept for Christians. Humans are free to choose between heaven and hell; time on earth is set for that purpose. To further explain relationship between the human person and God, God sees his human creation as his children, his family. Christians consider themselves to be brothers and sisters in Christ. This brother and sisterhood in the faith is unique to Christians. Calling God father to a Muslim could be extremely offensive.

The concept of what constitutes a human, original sin, guilt, and the effects of original sin, represent theological differences between Islam and Christians. Islam rejects Christian beliefs. Islam focuses on the whole human species, and not the individual. "MAN" is not burdened with an original sin. God, according to Islam, sees the whole human species as a unit. God governs the fate of the individual through human fate and divine predestination. Human salvation depends exclusively on the will of God and divine providence.

Metaphysical theories (the studies of being, existence, and reality) of Islam understand the human being to have been created as a species, and not created as an individual. Two prominent Arab philosophers of the Islamic tradition included Avicenna (980–1037 AD), and Averroes (1126–1198 AD). Averroes and Avicenna formed different interpretations of the Aristotelian theory of the intellect. What they said about the human mind and its ability to reason is important and has great significance. The human mind for Avicenna exists outside the specific soul, and for Averroes, there is one whole interpersonal mind.[99] For these philosophers, no individual being is able to reason independently. Reason is derived from a common source, as for example, information that may be filtered through a television antenna.

The Holy Trinity

Some philosophical concepts to be explored next include various aspects of the Holy Trinity. Christian doctrine states that Christ is 100% God and Christ is 100% man (a concept in which the human mind is unable to fathom. Christians accept this notion by faith). Christ had a divine nature and a human nature. Christ was only one person – the divine one.[100] These are difficult concepts for anyone to comprehend, and impossible for one of the Muslim faith. While some just consider the trinity to be a mystery, others try to understand it, comprehend it, and explain it. The trinity is a complicated and confusing subject. Let us now briefly outline the philosophical reasons supporting the Christian theses of the trinity in terms of faith.

One may attempt to explain these concepts, but only through the dogma of the holy trinity, and with metaphysics. For this, we turn to famous philosophers and theologians of the past, their hypothesis, how they conducted their research, and how they come to their conclusions.

St. Thomas Aquinas (1226 AD–1274 A.D.) is one famous philosopher and Christian theologian that will be referenced.[101] His explanations may

---

99 Władysław Tatarkiewicz, *Historia filozofii* [*History of Philosophy*], (Warszawa: Państwowe Wydawnictwo Naukowe, 1970), vol. 1, pp. 232–3.

100 Mieczyław A. Krąpiec, *Metaphysics. An Outline of the Theory of Being*, (New York: Peter Lang, 1991), pp. 297–8.

101 The Summa Theologiae was written between 1265–1274 A.D., and is also known as the Summa Theologica, or simply the Summa. It means a summary of theology. The Summa is the best-known work of Thomas Aquinas (c. 1225–1274 A.D.). Although unfinished, the Summa is "one of the classics of the history of philosophy, and one of the most influential works of Western literature". The Summa was intended to be used as an instructional guide for theology students, including seminarians and the literate laity. It is a compendium of all of the main theological teachings of the Catholic Church. It presents the reasoning for almost all points of Christian theology in the West. The Summa's topics follow a cycle: God; Creation, "MAN"; "MAN'S" purpose;

serve as an aide to comprehension. He studied scripture, prayed, attended a university in Naples, and wrote enough books of value to be considered noteworthy by one of the Christian faiths (Roman Catholic). He was named one of the twelve doctors or experts of the Catholic Church. He was named a saint.[102] Thomas Aquinas emphasizes in his description of God, that he as a triune God, and that this God is not alone.[103] Thomas interpreted the dogma (the officially established opinion) regarding the Holy Trinity, in two ways. One was by using metaphysical terminology and categories. The other was through the internal and spiritual life of a person, in the areas of love and cognition. This description is still minimal, when considering the immensity of God in the trinity. It does allow for a Triune God that can be discovered and understood, even if that understanding is to be minimal in terms of what the divine Trinity is. The Holy Trinity as understood by Christians, is the mystery about God existing simultaneously as three persons. This cannot be approached through common sense or traditional learning methods. Our common sense is shaped by the contact with the material world, whereas God is an absolutely spiritual being. Methods of learning about the material reality cannot be directly transferred to learning about the spiritual.

Moreover, while speaking about the Holy Trinity, we enter the sphere of theology, which employs philosophy, having its own terminology and categories. The philosophical system utilizes words, such as nature and substance, in describing the word trinity, which will have their own technical meaning to clarify concepts. Theological meanings cannot be taken arbitrarily. One needs to approach them with caution and sensitivity.[104]

Christ; the Sacraments; cycling theologically back to God. https://dhspriory. org/thomas/summa/.

102 The naming of a saint goes beyond the scope of this book. Briefly, in order to be named as a saint, one must have lived a worthy life, even if it meant overcoming great sin, serve as an example for future generations of Christian living, and to have miracles attributed to their intercession (their prayers to God, from heaven, on one's behalf).

103 Thomas Aquinas, *Summa Theologica* I, 31, 3, ad 1: 4 May 2018 http://www. corpuSumma Theologicaomisticum.org/iopera.html.

104 Latin: cum cautela et modestia, Aquinas, *Summa Theologica* I, 31, 2.

It is an extremely difficult concept for the human mind to fathom, God as three persons, a trinity. Some may explain it in simple terms, as one might the fingers on a hand, or, the leaves on a three-leaf clover... To a Christian, the three persons in God are meaningful. Also, one may explain it as follows: The love between the Father (God) and the Son (Jesus Christ) was so complete, that this Love became expressed as the Holy Spirit.

With the finite mind of humanity, people think numerically when they consider the concept of three in one persons. However, this is not a concept that can be reduced to a numerical equation. The Holy Trinity can be considered numerically in a metaphorical way only.[105] It denotes the number of beings remaining in the relationship with one another, three persons, together, all possessing one essence.[106] More theoretically, metaphysics is branch of philosophy that explores the nature of reality, answering questions including: what is there, and what is it like? Metaphysics may be a useful approach to apply here because the category of substance and the category of a person are metaphysical categories.

Examined through the study of metaphysics, three persons are not the same as three substances.[107] The difficulty in understanding the concept of the trinity may result from confusion between person and substance. The person is the most perfect form of existence, not to be treated as a substance.[108] The Holy Trinity refers to three persons, not three substances. The person directly denotes the relationship, and indirectly the essence. The situation is different when one considers the case of "MAN" as a person, since in the case of a "MAN", a person is an individual substance. The differences in God come from the different relations to the source. This relationship is not an accident, but the essence of God, and that's why it exists in itself. Person as related to God, means, relation as existing in itself, and not relation as a category of an accident, among other categories like space or time, what occurs in the case of relations conceived as categories of being in the world around us. And that is the reason why a person related to God means relation directly and an essence indirectly. This is what heretics

---

105 Aquinas, *Summa Theologica* I, 30, 3c.
106 Aquinas, *Summa Theologica* I, 31, 1, ad 1.
107 Aquinas, *Summa Theologica* I, 31, 1, ad 1.
108 Aquinas, *Summa Theologica* I, 29, 1c, 3c.

(people whose religious beliefs are in contrast with the fundamental beliefs of their church) did not consider, and as such, gave a false interpretation of the Trinity.[109]

When relation is treated as a substance, the Holy Trinity is a person. And since it is relation, in God there are different relations and there are three different persons.[110] It is not a plurality conceived in an absolute way, but a plurality of relations.[111] In God there are three relations: paternity (fatherhood), filiation (relationship between father and child), and procession (number in relation to the source).[112] Word (as obtained from the word of God, the Bible), comes in an intellectual way; the Holy Spirit comes in a way of love. The Trinity cannot be treated in a numerical way.[113] It is a number of persons who are, or, who are being in relation to each other.[114] There are three persons in one nature.[115]

There are two processions in God, love, and the word. These both take place in the Holy Trinity and under one simple act.[116] God loves His essence, in truth, and in goodness.[117] God can only be love, complete, total, and absolute. What is loved is in the loving one.[118]

The Word comes from God, in the form of cognition, as something perceived in the intellect. This operates inside the human person, as a thought, as something cognized in us. The Word of God is perfectly united with the one it stems from, between God and his creation.[119] The inner origin is perfect in character and allows us to be in unity with Him. *Procession* may refer to the Word, and *procession* may refer to the Holy Spirit. Both are in God and what is in God is God.[120] Some aspects of the mystery referring

---

109 Aquinas, *Summa Theologica* I, 29, 4c.
110 Aquinas, *Summa Theologica* I, 30, 1c.
111 Aquinas, *Summa Theologica* I, 30, 1, ad 3.
112 Aquinas, *Summa Theologica* I, 30, 2, ad 1.
113 Aquinas, *Summa Theologica* I, 30, 2, 3c.
114 Aquinas, *Summa Theologica* I, 31, 1 ad 1.
115 Aquinas, *Summa Theologica* I, 31, 1, ad 4.
116 Aquinas, *Summa Theologica* I, 27, 5, ad 3.
117 Aquinas, *Summa Theologica* I, 27, 5, ad 2.
118 Aquinas, *Summa Theologica* I, 27, 5, 3c.
119 Aquinas, *Summa Theologica* I, 27, 1, ad 2.
120 Aquinas, *Summa Theologica* I, 27, 3, ad 2.

to "procession" can only be explained in great detail, and only through the theory and study of metaphysics. For more detail, please refer to Thomas Aquinas, Summa Theologica.

To simplify this very confusing concept: God has put inside each one of his creation a seed of faith, a means of knowing him through the love that exists between God and his creation, and through the ability to learn, understand, and think. In the Christian faith, God thirsts for his creation, always finding ways to seek after and find, to form a relationship between himself and his creatures. This God eagerly waits for his creation to answer yes to his invitation, but will never intrude or force his will upon us. He patiently knocks at the door of his creatures. Because of free will and free choice, a person may continue to say no. God will continue to invite, never giving up. To contrast this with the faiths proclaiming a God that exists in the form of a solitary God, the God is selfishly waiting for creation to search for him.

Christians describe their faith as being rich, allowing for a personal lifetime of growth between humanity and creator. On the other hand, when Trinity is not explored using both metaphysical and spiritual descriptions, proper terms and theses, the idea of the Trinity can be neither defended nor understood. When metaphysical knowledge is missing, and when the only point of reference is the material world, the trinity cannot be comprehended on any level, as difficult as it is for any person.

Muslims reject the concept of the trinity, having a viewpoint that is common sense oriented, rather than mystery oriented. The rejection and criticism of the belief in the trinity, for example, found in the Islamic faith, may be due to either misunderstanding about what the trinity is, or, a rejection of teachings from theologians versed in this subject. They do not consider the deeper theological background presented by authors including St. Augustine or Thomas Aquinas, Christian philosophers who supported and explained the concept of the trinity that is accepted by Christian theology.

Determining Human Destiny

Key concepts may be explored to demonstrate differences in beliefs between various religious theologies. Some of these concepts include personalism; divine providence; free will, determinism, (freedom of choice versus fate); and predestination. When discussing the culture of Europe, differences

between Christians and Muslims may be demonstrated through the explo-
ration of these concepts.

Firstly, a review of terms is in order. These terms include: Predestination
(all events have been willed by God); free will (the freedom to choose for
oneself); determinism (the philosophical theory that everything including
moral choice is determined by previously existing causes); and providence.
The Latin word providence, translated from the Latin word accurately,
denotes the ability to see in advance what is going to happen. Providence
includes everything, Gods' care and guidance over everyone, every living
creature, everything).[121] Next, one may examine the differences between
predestination versus free will, and providence versus determinism.

Personalism

Christianity contributed the concept of personalism to the world cultural
heritage. Personalism views an individual as being unique and special,
because a supreme God created that person at conception. Personalism,
the idea of valuing all persons, is, by its very nature, universal (for everyone)
and trans-religious (everywhere, not solely in a church).

Islam theology does not accept the concept of personalism, because they
believe that the human person was created as a species and not as an individual (as discussed above.)

Human Choice: Free Will, or Determinism

Does the human person have free will, (the freedom to choose for oneself), and, if the person has free will, to what extent? Does a supreme God,
or fate, control the actions of the human person? These are important
questions to reflect upon.

Firstly, regardless of good and evil, what influence does the human will
have in directing human life? Secondly, what happens when human will
is ignored (fundamentalism, totalitarianism)? These questions arise from
concepts including: Is the issue of salvation crucial from the perspective of
human life? Or, are the perspectives of individual and social demoralization,

---

121 Aquinas, *Super Sent.*, lib. 1 d. 40 q. 1 a. 2 co: 4 May 2018 http://www.
corpusthomisticum.org/snp1001.html.

and liberalism, correct whereby the human will is not a factor regarding human salvation?

Christian philosophy believes in the concept of the human person as being unique. Christianity views a person as being endowed with its own intellect and free will. Free will is the ability to make choices that are not controlled by fate or by a supreme God. In the Islamic stance, it is impossible to call "MAN" a person, because Islam believes that there is a common intellect for all. This intellect is separate from individuals. For Islam, free will does not exist.

How do believers in fate deal with the problem of human free will, if a supreme God has already decided all? Christians postulate: Humans, to be free, need to have both and individual mind and an individual will.

The Christian stance is not uniform. There are thousands of protestant denominations, and within each denomination there are many different viewpoints. It is difficult to pinpoint one protestant doctrine regarding predestination and free choice. Calvinism will be used to discuss protestant theology, as it is the most dominant. Calvinism is closest to Islam in its viewpoints.

One Christian denomination, that of the Catholic Church, is clear about its doctrine. The Roman Catholic faith follows a church authority; any and all concepts are defined in a doctrine entitled: Catechism of the Catholic Church. In this document, beliefs are clearly formulated. Protestant denominations can also have clearly defined beliefs, if accessed through their respective churches, and on their respective web sites. For ease of discussion, one Christian stance will be selected, taken from catholic theology.

Divine Providence and Predestination

How are predestination, divine providence, and determinism, explained in the face of the free choice a human may experience? What makes a person human?

Since St Thomas Aquinas is considered one of the Catholic Church's greatest theologians and philosophers, the whole explication of the relation between free will, predestination, and providence, contained herein, is taken from St. Thomas, and will be explained as we progress through this book.

Thomas Aquinas proposed that human efforts are essential to achieve salvation (free will), although, God can save anyone due to His grace (predestination). In this discussion, predestination includes only those who have the free will. This attitude has religious, moral (for the individual and family), and political consequences. Religion puts pressure on humanity to do good and avoid evil. Without religion, morality loses its power. When salvation is independent of morality, degeneration of personal, social, and political life results. The doctrine of fate does not accept free will. Fate believes that uncontrollable and unforeseen forces direct a preordained life course regardless of human action. Islam follows the view that because of divine predestination, humans are missing the individual intellect. Islam views humans as not having freedom of choice, because there is one common intellect for all humanity, which exists apart from individual human beings. Christians may disagree: To be human, a person must possess both its own intellect and its own free will in order to be a complete human being. A person devoid of free will may not be defined as a person.

In the Islamic stance, humans, because they are missing the individual intellect, may not be considered to be a person. For a Christian, the problem lies in the fact that if all the things concerning the future have already been decided by God, there is no place for the human free will. It exerts influence on the concept of "MAN", because "MAN' devoid of free will is not a person. Human entity has to have both mind and will.

Divine Providence and its relationship to Predestination, is considered from a Christian Catholic perspective.[122] God's divine providence, and free will: One may wonder what and how these seemingly opposite concepts could be reconciled with each other? God directs and is in control, (divine order) towards his purpose (Predestination). Because God (as a divine order) is in control, one cannot change predestination. Predestination can however be strengthened or weakened.

God directs humankind (providence). Providence refers to everything. Predestination is a part of providence and includes secondary causes. Predestination includes anything that enhances human salvation. In a theological sense, predestination refers only to what exceeds the capacity of

---

122 „Praedestinatio est pars providentiae', Aquinas, *Summa Theologica* I, 23, 1–8.

human nature. More simply stated, God will intervene to assist someone when this person requires God's assistance and asks for it.[123]

God aids the human person only because of his grace, his glory, and his love. Predestination in a theological sense does not denote determinism. It portrays who, according to God's will, will be saved and who will not be. Humans are tested. Roman Catholics and some protestant denominations differ in their beliefs regarding salvation. According to Catholic doctrine, human effort is required for salvation, as contrasted with many protestant denominations, which believe that a human is saved when the person accepts Jesus Christ as Lord and savior into one's life.

God intervenes in the world. In theology God's intervention is given the term Divine Providence. The Latin word providence, translated from the Latin word accurately, denotes the ability to see in advance what is going to happen.[124]

God upholds the existence and general order of the universe, and may intervene in special ways, through for example, performing miracles in response to prayer. A supreme God created humanity. When he created the human person, he created in that person some qualities including: goodness, an inclination to reach a proper destiny, and a specific goal, a goal designed uniquely for that person alone.

Some further questions philosophers and theologians consider: What is the relationship between divine providence and the freedom to choose? How may free choice coincide with a providence that does not deprive man's freedom?

These questions may be answered from the following perspectives: Because God has a divine intellect, God is able to look forward into the future; God is able to accurately predict everything. Two distinctions (orders) are needed. The first order may be defined in this way: All things are subordinate to God. God can predict everything. The second order involves God's management and enforcement of all things that are subordinate to him. Intermediate levels within the second order complicate it. God governs the lower things by means of the higher ones. God is divine and good. Because

---

123 Latin: Providence: *Providentia*.
124 Aquinas, *Summa Theologica* I, 22, 1c.

of an excess of this goodness and his love, God grants causality to other beings, where the first is partly responsible for the second, and the second is partly dependent on the first.[125]

A peculiar situation takes place with respect to the human person, when considered from the viewpoint of Christian philosophers. Two factors may be considered when assessing whether something can be achieved or not. Whether something can be achieved is based upon the very nature of its being. The first factor: is a person able to achieve the purpose to which that person is created, based upon ones very nature, is it within that person's reach? If the purpose to which that person is created is beyond ones reach based upon that person's very nature, the second factor of analyses comes into play. When that person is unable to achieve their personal purpose because of their very nature, the acquisition of their personal purpose can be achieved if that person is guided by something else. Said in theological language: "MAN" is not able to achieve eternal life solely by the power of his own nature, and therefore God somehow guides it, pre-destination.[126] However, predestination[127] is not imposed upon "MAN", he has the option of reaching his purpose, and he retains freedom of his will.[128]

Three attitudes are significant regarding God's will, and predestination. At one end of the spectrum is the belief that magic could change the plans of God, with and without God's consent. Islam and protestant Calvinism fall at one extreme end of the spectrum, stressing that human behavior plays no role, towards human salvation. They are of the opinion that "MAN", as the human person, is completely helpless towards the ability to affect one's own salvation. In the opposite opinion of the Roman Catholic theologian, St Thomas Aquinas, "MAN" is a free being and is author of his own decisions and actions. He at the same time respected the superiority of God.

Christianity, through its attempt to understand philosophically, such interesting concepts including: humanity, free will, determination, and pre-destination, has reached a new stage of development. While beginning in Europe, Christianity has had an immeasurable effect upon Europe, and,

---

125 Aquinas, *Summa Theologica* I, 22, 1c.
126 Aquinas, *Summa Theologica* I, 22, 1c.
127 Latin: *destinatio* – directing.
128 Aquinas, *Summa Theologica* I, 22, 2c.

upon the rest of the world. Christianity gave the world a new understanding of God, creation, and of humanity. Not only does Christianity complete classical Greek and Roman culture, it exceeds it immeasurably. Christianity allowed Europe to advance to the highest level of cultural development. An understanding of humanity may be viewed not only from the field of the world and technology, but from the entire universe and God. The creation of humanity has a universal dimension due to a universal mission. Moreover, it is due to Christianity that the peoples inhabiting Europe gain the sense of community and European identity.[129]

Historical Responses to Evangelization

The method of encouraging others to accept the faith is contrasted between the Christian perspectives compared with Islam's approach. A key difference exists between Islam and Christianity regarding their methods of spreading of the faith. Christians believe that a loving God wants his followers (disciples), to be a witness and to be a demonstration of God's love. Having been forgiven by God, Christians are to forgive others and forgive one self.

Pope Benedict XVI (Pope of the Catholic Church between 2005 and 2013) discussed methods of the propagation of faith for Christian Catholics. In one of his lectures (Regensburg), he cited a conversation between a representative of the Byzantine emperor and a representative of Islam. The Emperor, having a Greek education, stated that faith could not be spread by violence, because violence complied neither with the nature of God nor with the nature of the soul. He added that people would be more willing to accept faith through reason, rather than through violence.[130]

The attitude to faith is a sign of the acceptance or rejection of freedom and human rationality. When faith is enforced, both freedom and rationality are diminished or even rejected.

One must emphasize that many Muslims are loving and peaceful. However, when looking at the Muslim holy reference book called the

---

129 Dawson, *Europe and the Seven Stages,* p. 134.
130 Benedict XVI, *Faith*: 4 May 2018 https://w2.vatican.va/content/benedict-xvi/en/speeches/2006/september/documents/hf_ben-xvi_spe_20060912_university-regensburg.html.

Koran, there are at least ten places in the Koran about jihad. Jihad means to convert those who do not follow the Muslim faith. Jihad is written in the Koran, it is not an extremist view of the Muslim faith.[131,132] Islam believes that faith should be spread by any means possible, ranging from peaceful methods up to military violence. Islam is a faith that believes in force to impose the faith. The word in the Muslim Koran to describe the force used to impose the faith of Islam is "Jihad". On an individual level the differences between Christianity and Islam may not be easily recognized. People living out both religions may demonstrate loving, peaceful, respectful behaviors.

Today, many Muslim countries express hostile attitudes towards Christians through persecutions and the threat to human life. In some of these countries, the public expression of faith in Jesus Christ is punished by death. The Jihad (as expressed in the Koran) is not only anti-Christian, but also anti anyone who is not Muslim. The Jihad expresses the following requirements: to kill those who leave the faith of Islam, and to wage war and subjugate non-Muslims in order that these peoples may come under Islamic law.

Close inspection of the teachings of Islam is imperative when societies choose universal acceptance of Islam teachings and practices into their country. Countries that do express hostile attitudes towards non-Muslims include, for example, Afghanistan, Saudi Arabia, Brunei, Egypt, Indonesia, Iran, Pakistan, Somalia, Sudan, and Syria.[133]

The newly proclaimed Islamic state (20.06.2014), in which the sharia law is in force, has proven to be especially dangerous for Christians. Sharia law is an Islamic religious law that is enforced by the whole power of the state administration.

There is no one Islam. There are however, many ways in which the Jihad may be interpreted, understood, and implemented. Not all Muslim

---

131 See footnote 134 for specific references concerning the jihad in the Koran.

132 One may argue that the Bible also references retribution behavior. It must be emphasized that the Old Testament is not the New One! The New Testament requires Christians to love your enemies. The worst scriptural dialogue is to jump from one quotation to another. This creates a lot of misunderstanding and manipulation regarding biblical texts.

133 Krzysztof Kościelniak, *Dżihad. Święta wojna w islamie* [*Jihad. Holy War in Islam*], (Kraków: Wydawnictwo "M", 2002), pp. 111–21.

sectors enforce the Jihad in an extremely aggressive manner. Jihad may be dangerous when extremists enforce an extreme interpretation of the law. Nevertheless, the militant Islam has dominated Islam and Islamic activity for centuries. Today, the enforcement of jihad often repeatedly occurs in an especially bloody way. When it comes to the Islamic jihad, we tackle the sensitive issue regarding the place and the role of conscience in accepting or rejecting religion.

The jihad denotes the effort undertaken to strengthen and expand Islam in the struggle to convert non-believers. It may take various forms, both peaceful and military. Texts of the Koran do support coercion and violence, although this is controversial.[134] Historically, when Islam first appeared, it elbowed its way through the sword, conquering a number of Christian lands. In the year 638 A.D., the Muslims conquered Jerusalem, Antioch and Caesarea. In the year 643 A.D., they conquered Alexandria, then northern Africa and Persia. In the thirteenth century, the Ottoman Empire appeared on the scene, giving a new impetus to the expansion of Islam. Constantinople was conquered and the Byzantine Empire fell.[135]

---

134 "... reading of this book [Koran] indicates at least 10 fragments that call for or justify violence." Krzysztof Kościelniak, *Dżihad*. p. 7. The following are the most important texts: „So you did not slay them, but it was Allah Who slew them, and you did not smite when you smote (the enemy), but it was Allah Who smote, and that He might confer upon the believers a good gift from Himself; surely Allah is Hearing, Knowing.' (VIII, 17); „So when the sacred months have passed away, then slay the idolaters wherever you find them, and take them captives and besiege them and lie in wait for them in every ambush, then if they repent and keep up prayer and pay the poor-rate, leave their way free to them; surely Allah is Forgiving, Merciful.' (IX, 5); 'If the hypocrites and those in whose hearts is a disease and the agitators in the city do not desist, We shall most certainly set you over them, then they shall not be your neighbours in it but for a little while; Cursed: wherever they are found they shall be seized and murdered, a (horrible) murdering.' (XXXIII, 60–61). Other fragments: II, 190–191; II, 216; IV, 74; VIII, 12; IX, 5; IX, 36; IX, 73; XXII, 39; XLVIII, 16; XLVII, 4; XLIX, 15; LXI, 4; LXVI, 9 (s. 24–31). In this context the fragment of "There is no compulsion in religion" (II, 256) is an exception, pp. 24–31. Maurice Gaudefroy-Demombynes, *Mahomet. L'homme et son message* (Paris: Albin, 1957).
135 Kościelak, *Dżihad*. pp. 50–5.

In the context of jihad, the philosophical and theological question remains: who is "MAN" at the most basic level? Is the human person intelligent and free or not? This is important to know.

What are the implications of forcing faith upon a person or nation? Again, as seen from a Christian perspective: When a person is a person, that person has the feature of being free and rational. The free person has the ability to use reason in ultimate matters relating to the recognition or the rejection of God.

The person, on whom faith can be forced through violence, is not treated as a human person. If humans are seen as having reason and freedom to choose, then coercion concerning faith negates these principles. If a lie were considered to be wrong, then a God, who could lie in order to express the mightiness of his power and will, would be a non-divine God.

Back through history, some Christians also used forceful methods in order to obtain conversions. Pagans, especially the Prussians, were converted by means of the fire and sword. For instance, one military warlike order that was used was entitled the Teutonic Order. Even in baptized countries, including Poland and Lithuania, the Imperial Policy was implemented under the pretext of conversion. The Imperial Policy dealt with an authority rule of a nation over dependent ones. Coercion and force did not prove to be an effective method of evangelization.

At the Council of Constance in Europe (1414 – 1418), Polish professors played a crucial role in stopping the practice of conversion by force, by presenting political and theological arguments against its practice.[136]

A Religion to Destroy Christianity

Theistic religion is a true religion, because it accepts religion as related to God. Atheism rejects God, and because of this, it may not be classified as a religion. A religion that is given little attention, is Theistic Satanism, the anti-Christian religion. This religion is based upon the worship of Satin, by perhaps, some people who feel angry or let down by God. There are

---

136 Key role was fullfilled by Paweł Włodkowic (Paul Wladimiri, 1370/3–1435). *Pisma wybrane Pawła Włodkowica. Works of Paul Wladimiri. A Selection)*, ed. Ludwik Ehrlich (Warszawa: Instytut Wydawniczy PAX, 1968), 3 volumes.

Satanic Priests. Materials used in satanic worship include those from the Catholic Church, if they can obtain them, (such as the bread from holy communion), in order to cause harm to Jesus Christ and his followers. Actual satanic rituals are practiced. The goal of satanic worshippers is to destroy the Christian church. Christians believe Satin was first mentioned in the book of Genesis, with Adam and Eve. Satin is mentioned numerous times throughout Christian scripture. Christians strongly believe Satin's influence continues until this day, creating havoc, turmoil, disease, marital discord – the evil in this present age.

IV. Europe: The Enlightened and the Backward

The Influence of religion upon culture continues. Divisions develop within Christianity, De Hellenization begins. The protestant reformation brought about a variety of changes in values, behaviors, and politics. What was once a Christian—Catholic belief system and practice, was disputed and radically changed. The emergence of the Protestant reformation had an impact on the European identity, as it once knew itself to be. European culture continued to be focused upon a Christian identity, yet a different one. Although Europe continued to be a Christian Europe, things changed.

Western Christianity in Crisis

At one time, Christianity was the distinguishing feature of being European. In modern times, this is no longer the case. Two significant historical factors have influenced this change. Through the Protestant Reformation, Christian identity and prestige came into question. Secondly, due to geographical discoveries at the turn of the fifteenth and sixteenth centuries, Christianity began to be practiced in other continents. Christianity ceased to be a purely European phenomenon.

Due to the influence of the Protestant reformation, there was no longer a common Christian religious and cultural dimension. Although Christianity continues to be the norm, Catholicism and Protestantism differ in religious, ethical, political, anthropological, and metaphysical perspectives. Each Christian denomination is clear regarding its beliefs, yet there is variation among denominations. There are currently thousands of protestant denominations each with their own belief system. Most of these denominations share in a uniform belief of the divinity of Jesus Christ, Jesus being the Son of God. With Christian belief systems, the Bible forms a foundation of the faith. Beyond this, there are a variety of perspectives within Christianity. When one considers whether Europeanness is Christianity, one is forced to wonder which form of Christianity?[137] What is important

---

137 This work is one of philosophy. The protestant reformation created a variety of problems related to the culture of Europe, which is to be discussed. At

is the controversy in its historical context. What happens today in the thousands of protestant sects becomes impossible to recognize. In some Christian churches, it is impossible to understand that the worship service in question might be Christian.

With the protestant reformation came an essential change in behavior, and a difference in the understanding of religious and moral principles. Protestant Christians no longer accepted the beliefs and practices of the Christian Catholic faith.

In an examination of the division between Christianity as practiced in the Roman Catholic right, and the beliefs and practices as generated through the Protestant reformation, there are key differences in belief and practice. Transubstantiation is one example, whereby Catholics believe that Jesus Christ becomes truly present: mind, body, soul and divinity, during a Catholic worship service. Other traditional beliefs and practices of Catholicism discarded by some Protestants included what happens during a worship service; purgatory (a cleansing after death of the soul, required by some prior to entering heaven); asking saints who are in heaven for prayer on the behalf of humans; asking for and honoring the assistance from Jesus's mother, Mary; Mary's place as the mother of God; the authority and infallibility of the Pope in matters of faith and morals; the role of the priest; sacraments (an outward sign of inward and spiritual divine grace); the succession of Christ's mission and priesthood through apostolic succession; and the concept of justice and mercy. The Catholic idea of justice and

---

one time, Christianity was united. Divisions began with orthodoxy in the years 1000 A.D. Then the Christian church became further divided in the 1500's with the protestant reformation. Both these periods of history saw many problems in the Roman Catholic Church, leading to the divisions. It is beyond the scope of this work to outline all these difficulties. Nor is the intent of the authors to advocate any Christian religion over another. All Christians desire unity. All the denominations offer something wonderful to the Christian faith. People in all denominations can be devote, and live exemplary lives of faith, love and service. It is therefore necessary to make strong mention that this work is not to discredit any of the Christian brothers or sisters in any denomination. What it is meant to discuss, is the philosophical changes that came as a result of the reformation that influenced culture. We leave the reader to determine whether these changes were to the detriment or benefit of the Christian family.

mercy is based upon rational and free will, which is enriched by virtue, and is open to the supernatural grace of God. A belief in predestination in the theological sphere motivates human conduct towards salvation. The human person may influence whether or not that human person will be saved through deeds, as well as through a conscious choosing to a accept God.[138]

Many Protestants replaced the above-mentioned Catholic beliefs with different ones. For many Protestants, beliefs changed to include: the total primacy of faith (sola fide) (only faith matters, not reason); the Bible alone is the basis of faith (sola scriptura); and a guarantee of salvation stemming from a belief in Jesus Christ as God.

As Protestantism became more prominent in Europe, human behavior, values, and politics began to change. Since Protestant "MAN" has no influence on being saved or not through deeds, he can put more emphasis upon his own needs and desires. Human behavior began to be guided through a focus on self instead of others, and egoism (pleasure seeking and self fulfilment). Philosophical and ethical European liberalism began to guide human behavior in ethics, and other fields of culture, especially in economics and politics.[139]

Protestant thinking greatly influenced changes in perceptions that were previously held in Catholicism. This caused a cultural shift in thinking which affected the concept of "MAN" (humanity), metaphysics, anthropology, and ontology. In the field of anthropology, (human societies, culture and their development), the Protestant image of a person, according to Luther, is a person who is an imperfect creature whose nature, as a result of the original sin, was completely broken.[140] The human will was believed to be too weak to do good. The powers of cognition were viewed as being

---

138 George P. Morse and Gerard J. Marks, *Précis of Official Catholic Teaching* (Washington D.C.: Catholic Committed to Support the Pope, 1990–2006) with Magisterial and Ecclesiastical approval and support, clear, concise and orthodox summaries of Roman Catholic Church teaching consisting of twelve volumes, taking 20 years to compile. The volumes are in use for teaching, research, and education by clergy and laity in over 50 countries.

139 Max Weber, *The Protestant Ethics and the Spirit of Capitalism*, trans. T. Parsons (London: Routlege, 1992), chapter 2.

140 Jacques Maritain, *Three Reformers. Luther, Descartes Rousseau* (London: Sheed and Ward, 1950), pp. 9–11.

too imperfect to cognize, to be aware of the reality. Because of this view-point, human authorities were seen as being ineffective in the performance of their specific activities, causing internal disintegration. Ontology (the branch of metaphysics dealing with the nature of possible being), became the branch of metaphysics that prevailed in the philosophical field. Reality lost its focus as the main subject of philosophy, replaced by the possible being.[141] Protestantism strengthened the agnostic and the idealistic tenden-cies present in European philosophy.

Due to the Protestant reformation, Europe lost its identity as a Christian culture. Europe developed a new identity. Civilization (as an idea) became the new European identity, replacing the previous Christian identity.

Toward the Ideology of Progress

Europe and Civilization became linked. European civilization continued to develop through further developments and progress. The word Ideology represents a negative connotation to the development of European culture. In general, the word ideology has a negative meaning. The word Theology in itself is neutral. The neutral word theology was invented by ancient Greeks, including Plato and Aristotle, as a theory about what is supposed to be divine.

The ideology of Enlightened Europe has many implications. The word Ideology is a neologism, a recent word that is in the process of entering common use, but has not fully been accepted into mainstream language. It was invented at the end of the eighteenth century in the context of the French Revolution[142], and was adapted later by Marxism. In France it meant the lowest theory of sensual cognition; in Marxism it has been an aprioristic project (doctrine of knowledge based upon reason or presupposed by expe-rience). The concept is about the idea that a new human, and a new society, is based upon basic values including personalism, family, and nation. The

---

141 Pius Brosch, *Die Ontologie des Johannes Clauberg* (Greifswald: Druck von E. Hartmann, 1926), pp. 20–2.
142 **Antoine-Louis-Claude, Comte Destutt de Tracy,** (1754–1836), French Philosopher and soldier, founded the school of ideology (https://www.brittanica.com).

word Ideology implies being against tradition, which many religions base their truths upon.

When one examines the negative implications of the word ideology further: in the name of an idea, (including perfect person or perfect society), ideology allows for the killing and destruction of mass groups of people. Genocide is an example of human cleansing in the name of an ideology of perfection. An ideology that serves as an idea of progress, allows for the fight against religion. Religion does not believe in a paradise on earth, as does atheism. Ideology of earth's perfection treats religion as the main obstacle to realizing its new paradise. Atheist communism persecuted, tortured and killed both Roman Catholic and Orthodox Christians in Russia because of their stance against atheism.[143] Atheism was, and continues to be against any religion.

The word "civilization" is a fairly new word (a neologism). In the English language, the word civilization began in the second half of the eighteenth century. The meaning and role of civilization in Europe has been in progress since the time of the Renaissance, the fifteenth, to the seventeenth Centuries.[144]

The late seventeenth and eighteenth Centuries saw an intellectual movement termed as the Enlightenment. Tradition lost its importance. Instead, reason and individualism became important during the age of the enlightenment. Philosophers such as Locke, Descartes and Newton heavily influenced its development. Europe developed a new self – consciousness, reaching its highest point (its apogee) during the time of the Enlightenment. Europe became a civilization. Civilization is now European Civilization, they are now one in the same.[145]

How is it possible for "Civilization", and "European civilization", to mean one and the same thing? Let's consider the history of philosophy that

---

143 Piotr Jaroszyński, *Science in Culture*, trans. Hugh McDonald (Amsterdam – New York: Rodopi, 2007), chapters 30–1.

144 The word *civilization* was coined based on the Latin word *civis* (citizen). It appears for the first time in the work written by Victor de Riquetti de Mirabeau *L'ami des hommes, ou traité de la population* (Avignon, 1759).

145 Juan R. Goberna Faique, *Civilización. Historia de una idea* (Universidad de Santiago de Compostela: Servicio de Publicacións e Intercambio Científico, 1999), pp. 34–51.

was evolving during the Enlightenment. New nations were being discovered; and new worlds were explored through geographical discoveries. Humanity inhabited the earth, not as a compact whole, but instead, humanity was spread among many people living on different continents.

A humanitarian focus was at the heart of the Europeans of the Enlightenment. Although the stage of development differed among nations, all peoples belonged to one human family. This brought about a perception of responsibility from those who were at the higher levels of development, namely Europe, to assist those at lower levels. Europe became a leader in the sphere of civilization. Hence, civilization became synonymous with the European civilization.[146] Being so highly evolved also meant a challenge to continue developing to a peak level of perfection, along a path called progress.

Europe's desire at the end of the fifteenth century, to bring civilization to the newly discovered people of other nations, had a strong ideological basis. The colonization by the Europeans of the Enlightenment is viewed in today's standards as exploitation.

Europe was comprised of many nations, who disagreed in terms of culture and level of development. Rivalry for supremacy began. Because the French coined the word civilization, civilization became identified with the French culture. Conflicts of ideologies, and rivalry, soon developed among the European nations for the top cultural position, leading to military wars. This culminated in the outbreak of the First World War. Europe was no longer seen as a leader of progress. The ideology of Euro centrism (interpreting the world through European or Anglo–American values and experiences) collapsed.[147]

The main driving force for the development of European civilization after the eighteenth century became reason applied to science. In fact, if it weren't for the European desire to excel in the realm of science, the achievements that we know today would not have occurred. The goal of scientific thought and development beginning at the time of the Renaissance became practical

---

146 Robert Nisbet, *Historia de la idea de progreso* (Barcelona: España, 1981), pp. 22–3.
147 Dawson, *Europe and the Seven Stages*, p. 148.

and useful (utilitarian), which was unique and distinct from the previous theoretical Greek model.[148]

The European scientific model fit perfectly with the mathematical model of cognition. Experience and experimentation were implemented into the field of scientific research, immensely contributing to the development of the scientific field. The image of Europe greatly changed, and then progressed throughout the world.

The spectacular successes of scientific knowledge, led to the industrial revolution in the nineteenth century, which in turn paved the way for the development of technology. A technique, which focused upon useful and practical information, began to have an impact upon a wider range of culture. More people were able to access an improved education. The welfare of society and its people improved.

Organized political communities under one government (the state) began to have more internal power, effectively controlling its citizens towards a unified whole. This had both positive and negative repercussions. Democracy was a positive factor. However, the final result of this change became negative. People agreed to give all of their individual rights to the state.

Practical and useful scientific research was one great contribution, in today's standards, that arose from Europe. This research is used to currently define progress, which continues to form a modern concept of Europeanism. A French revolutionary and Enlightenment author, Marie-Jean-Antoine-Nicolas Caritat, Marquis de Condorcet, wrote a short and significant book entitled "Outlines of an Historical View of the Progress of the Human Mind" [1795].[149] In this text (which is well worth the readers further reading), he explained that Europe did in fact have an important and significant role in spreading civilization and progress. He made two significant points. Firstly, when one is able to compare what will happen in the natural world to the future of humanity, one can predict the future

---

148 Paolo Rossi, *Francis Bacon. From Magic to Science*, trans. Sacha Rabinovitch (Chicago: University of Chicago Press, 1978), pp. 1–7.

149 Marie-Jean-Antoine-Nicolas Caritat, Marquis de Condorcet, *Outlines of an Historical View of the Progress of the Human Mind, Being a Posthumous Work of the Late M. de Condorcet* (Philadelphia: M. Carey, 1796): 5 May 2018 http://oll.libertyfund.org/titles/1669.

of humanity. Laws governing universal phenomena including the necessity and permanence of universal rights can be derived from knowledge of natural sciences. Secondly, science enhances one's ability to acquire knowledge and understanding through thought, which in turn enhances possibilities for intellectual development, and increases one's moral capacity.[150]

According to Condorcet, true equality is the ultimate goal of all social organization, and is an indicator of development and true civilization.[151] Improvement of humanity required the overthrow of the inequalities between nations, and greater equality within the same nation.[152] This is what truly defined civilization. The French and Anglo – Americans truly realized this concept as they aimed to eliminate internal and external inequality. Other nations may be lagging behind this ideal in terms of civilization.

Intellectual growth and development became a focus of progress. The mind was viewed as the most important strength that humans possess. The human mind has a capacity to direct human conduct, to assist humans in order to satisfy human needs, and to allow people to recognize and act upon knowledge of human rights. To be strong, the mind needed to be free of superstition. Perfection of the intellect could be achieved through the perfection of physical and human ability, the development of the sciences and arts, and improving the instruments which augmented human power.[153]

The principles set forth in the French constitution most thoroughly defined civilization, and, according to Condorcet, would be a useful model for the development of other civilizations. Condorcet believed that the French constitution included principles that expressed what it meant to be civilized and enlightened. Equality was thoroughly defined. For Condorcet, the Nations that would be ready to accept the principles of the French constitution were Enlightened Europeans. These nations would thereby be ready to accept civilization.[154]

The Europe of the Enlightenment provided two universal achievements to civilization, firstly the development of sciences and arts, and secondly the

---

150 Condorcet, *Outlines*, Tenth Epoch.
151 Condorcet, *Outlines*, Tenth Epoch.
152 Condorcet, *Outlines*, Tenth Epoch.
153 Condorcet, *Outlines*, Tenth Epoch.
154 Condorcet, *Outlines*, Tenth Epoch.

constitutional and real principle of equality among people. Gradually these principles became accepted in Europe, and then were accepted in the whole inhabited world. The Europe of the enlightenment believed that a law of nature can be applied to plants and animals, as well as the human species. This law of nature implied that a society must develop or degenerate.[155] Europe of the Enlightenment also believed that, in order for humanity to progress, it must follow the principles of the Enlightenment. If it did not follow these rules, humanity was doomed to degenerate.

The ideology of Enlightened Europe was to move toward what it believed to be progress. This movement created a momentum toward a direction of change in Europe, and a direction for change in the world in general. This change entailed removing the obstacles that interfered with progress. These obstacles included the monarchy, in their perspective to be a bad political system, and religion, especially Christianity. Values and principles promoted through Christianity, clash with values and principles propagated by a world view of relativism and egotism. This clash inevitably could propagate an anti- Christian stance.

Enlightened Europe promoted an ideology which people hoped would guarantee development, prosperity and peace through democracy and secularization.

De-Hellenization of Europe

Anti-Hellenism (against Greek culture) became a strong force in response to Greek enculturation, which in turn affected the Christian culture of Europe.

As Alexander the Great's army conquered foreign peoples, Greek culture, religion and language spread over Europe (Hellenization). In opposition to this, anti–Hellenism developed, whereby the value of Greek culture was questioned. The Greek culture was thought of as a threat. Anti–Hellenism became the first manifestation of Anti Occidentalism–anti Western senti-ment. (Anti Greece became the first form of anti-western attitudes).

In ancient times, the Jewish religion may have attempted to defend itself through a sentiment of anti–Hellenism. This anti Hellenism may not have been, for them, a fight against a European identity.

---

155 Condorcet, *Outlines*, Tenth Epoch.

There were three phases of anti–Hellenism to notice. The first phase lasted from the sixteenth century to the times of Kant (1724–1804), the second appears in the nineteenth century, together with Adolf von Harnack (1873–1912), and the third one includes the contemporary or the present time.[156]

European identity could have been affected however, by anti–Hellenism within protestant Christianity, according to Pope Benedict XVI. Pope Benedict XVI may become known in time as a great philosopher and theologian of the twenty first century. He attributed the anti–Hellenization movement that was brought about through Protestantism, to a desire to cleanse faith of elements brought about from philosophy. Why philosophy? Philosophy was a product of the Greek pagan culture, making it an expression of the pagan spirit. In order to find pure faith, one was required to turn towards the Revelation contained in the Scriptures. While the catholic tradition relies on scripture and tradition, Protestantism focused upon scripture only, sola Scriptura. For Protestants, the content of faith was to be found only in the Bible, the Scripture, and not in a (metaphysical) philosophical system. According to Protestants, the system, one of a known tradition, was created by pagans, and served to deform faith.

Philosophers including Kant expressed the first phase of anti-Hellenism. Immanuel Kant was an influential philosopher who contributed to metaphysics and ethics. Kant supported the concept of eliminating the traditional aspects of worship, and replacing them with ethics only. Kant also concluded that the theoretical cognition of philosophy must be removed from faith in order to preserve it. The only place for faith is in the moral order, which is central to culture in that it defines good, right and virtuous behavior, through having a practical mind.[157]

Enlightened Europe saw some other strong movements developing. These movements included: removing the Greek influence from the world, and removing faith from philosophy. Next, the focus became removing

---

156 Benedict XVI, *Faith*.

157 Kant discussed a purely practical rational faith, referring to the meaning of faith in the moral order and in the moral order only. Immanuel Kant, *The Critic of Practical Reason*, trans. Thomas Kingsmill Abbott (Project Gutenberg): 4 May 2018 http://www.gutenberg.org/ebooks/5683, I, 2, 8.

paganism and mythology from philosophical thinking, because Greek culture was still at the forefront of philosophical thinking. For the Greeks, the mind was at the center of human life. Thinking, especially theoretical thinking, was the activity that separated humans from other creatures. The mind was at the center and particular to human life, penetrating all spheres of human life, including morality and religion.

On the contrary, mythology was seen by the educated Greeks as an obstacle to philosophical reasoning, due to its staggering premises. Aristotle was one philosopher who aimed to remove mythology from Greek philosophical systems, especially in the pre Socrates era. Theoretical thinking was not to be influenced by paganism or pagan premises, which had as its roots mythology. Some elements of mythology did remain in the Greek philosophical systems as an attempt to overcome it, recognizing that some mythology may present an important basis for reasoning and philosophizing.[158] Paganism did present a theoretical category. The Christian worldview sometimes argues that pagan mythology rejected Christ because he was not depicted in stories nor was he included.[159] This thinking was in

---

158 Aristotle, *Metaphysics*, III, 1000a 9–22.

159 "The word heresy as stated in the first objection denotes a choosing. Now choice as stated above (FS, Question [13], Article [3]) is about things directed to the end, the end being presupposed. Now, in matters of faith, the will assents to some truth, as to its proper good, as was shown above (Question [4], Article [3]): wherefore that which is the chief truth, has the character of last end, while those which are secondary truths, have the character of being directed to the end.

Now, whoever believes, assents to someone's words; so that, in every form of unbelief, the person to whose words assent is given, seems to hold the chief place and to be the end as it were; while the things by holding which one assents to that person hold a secondary place. Consequently, one that holds the Christian faith as being right, assents, by freewill, to Christ, in those things which truly belong to the doctrine of Christ.

Accordingly there are two ways in which someone may deviate from the rectitude of the Christian faith. First, because of an unwillingness to assent to Christ. Such a person has an evil will, so to say, in respect of the very end. This belongs to the species of unbelief in pagans and the Jewish. Secondly, because, though intending to assent to Christ, fails in the free choice of those things wherein one assents to Christ, because that person chooses not what Christ really taught, but the suggestions of one's own mind. Thomas Aquinas, *Summa Theologica* II-II, 11, 1c.

error. The classical Greek philosophy was not pagan due to the fact that Christ, as we knew him in human form, was not present in the world at the time of creation.

As we move into the nineteenth and twentieth centuries, the second phase of anti-Hellenism, appeared. Liberal theology became the new trend in philosophical thinking, growing from the Enlightenment and protestant thinking. Liberal theology has no set of unified beliefs. It promotes the idea that theology and philosophy should be removed from faith. The benefit of Greek philosophy is that it provided the tools to interpret Scripture in the theological and in the moral dimension.

For Enlightened Europe, and protestant thinking, biblical stories are thought of metaphorically in order to emphasize moral and spiritual lessons. It is left to the individual to decipher the meaning of scripture. A roman catholic, or a philosopher, would disagree with the reliability of individual interpretation of scripture. Both groups question whether the individual is capable of providing a good interpretation to scripture, when the content of the Revelation was presented in an analogical form and metaphor.[160] The many thousands of protestant churches in existence may highlight the disparity that comes from this personal interpretation of scripture. Liberal theology also presents Christ in scripture as not being God, but a human being, perhaps a prophet, who provided messages to humanity, and a humanitarian approach to life. Christ, rather than being God, becomes thought of as the father of humanitarianism, (a movement respecting and providing for human rights and needs).[161]

---

160 Mieczysław A. Krąpiec, *Filozofia w teologii [Philosophy in Theology]*, (Lublin: Instytut Edukacji Narodowej, 1999), pp. 5–8.

161 The liberal theology of the nineteenth and twentieth centuries ushered in a second stage in the process of Dehellenization, with Adolf von Harnack (Baltic German Lutheran 1851-1930) as its outstanding representative. This program was highly influential in Catholic theology during Pope Benedict's (nee Ratzinger) early years as a student and early years of teaching. Liberal theology took as its point of departure Blaise Pascal's (Christian French Philosopher 1623 – 1662) distinction between the God of the philosophers, and the God of Abraham, Isaac and Jacob. In Pope Benedict's inaugural lecture at Bonn in 1959, he addressed the issue about this second stage of DE Hellenization. According to Benedict, "Harnack's central idea was to return simply to the man Jesus and to his simple message. Underneath the accretions of theology

The third phase of anti-Hellenism continues into our present time. Historically, Christianity formed part of the dominant Greek culture. Christianity and Greek philosophy formed an historical connection. Following the conquests of Alexander the Great, Greek was the language most used by the different nations who were influenced by the Greek culture. The New Testament (the part of the Bible concerning Christ's life and deeds) was written in the Greek language. (Koiné)

Inculturation (the term used by Roman Catholics), or contextual theology (the term used by protestants), was used to describe church teachings that were adapted and presented to non-Christian cultures, the aim being to influence both cultures. Because the dominant Greek culture included Christian inculturation, contextual theology, was believed to be needed.

The dominance of the Greek culture was time limited. Enlightened Europe believed that both the Greek culture and Christianity were unnecessary in our present time. Currently, when Christian believers present Christianity to other cultures, care and attention is paid to the specific peoples, the Greek context is disregarded.[162]

---

and indeed of Hellenization: this simple message was seen as the culmination of the religious development of humanity. Jesus Christ's purpose on earth was to be one of morality, not worship. In the end he was presented as the father of a humanitarian moral message." Benedict XVI. The full lecture may be found at   *Faith*.   http://www.catholic-ew.org.uk/Home/News/2006/2006-Offline/Full-Text-of-the-Pope-Benedict-XVI-s-Regensburg-Lecture

162 „Dehellenization first emerges in connection with the postulates of the Reformation in the sixteenth century. Looking at the tradition of scholastic theology, the Reformers thought they were confronted with a faith system totally conditioned by philosophy, that is to say an articulation of the faith based on an alien system of thought. As a result, faith no longer appeared as a living historical Word but as one element of an overarching philosophical system. The principle of sola scriptura, on the other hand, sought faith in its pure, primordial form, as originally found in the biblical Word. Metaphysics appeared as a premise derived from another source, from which faith had to be liberated in order to become once more fully itself. When Kant stated that he needed to set thinking aside in order to make room for faith, he carried his program forward with a radicalism that the Reformers could never have foreseen. He thus anchored faith exclusively in practical reason, denying it access to reality as a whole. [...] Before I draw the conclusions to which all this has been leading, I must briefly refer to the third stage of dehellenization, which

Benedict XVI responded to the latest manifestation of anti-Hellenism in his Regensburg lecture.[163] He shed some insights upon the importance of the New Testament having been written in Greek. Language leaves an imprint. There are ways of saying some things in one language that cannot be said as effectively in another. The Greek culture and language reached a high level of intellectual maturity.

According to Pope Benedict, Christianity benefitted from that maturity of language, education, reason, and rationality. It does not mean however that at the same time Christianity was pressed to accept the Greek image of the world. The change of the image of the world was done because of the Revelation and reason itself. Christianity was able to discard aspects of the Greek image of the world that were anachronic, naïve or philosophically unmatured. The world image was changing. It changed due to the Revelation of scripture, and because of the impact of reason (philosophy and science). The important influence of the Greek spirit was hard to deny. Benedict's impression was both important and philosophically sound: "The New Testament was written in Greek. The fundamental decisions made about the relationship between faith and the use of human reason, are part of faith."[164]

For those who support the theology of the Christian faith, the Greek culture provided a positive influence, and not a deformation of faith. Greek philosophy facilitated a Christian identity to develop. Through its inherent nature of being open to self-improvement, philosophy provided

---

is now in progress. In the light of our experience with cultural pluralism, it is often said nowadays that the synthesis with Hellenism achieved in the early Church was an initial inculturation which ought not to be binding on other cultures." Benedict XVI, *Faith*.

163   Benedict XVI, *Faith*.

164   "This thesis [that Hellenism has only historical meaning] is not simply false, but it is coarse and lacking in precision. The New Testament was written in Greek and bears the imprint of the Greek spirit, which had already come to maturity as the Old Testament developed. True, there are elements in the evolution of the early Church, which do not have to be integrated into all cultures. Nonetheless, the fundamental decisions made about the relationship between faith and the use of human reason are part of the faith itself; they are developments consonant with the nature of faith itself." Benedict XVI, *Faith*.

an effective and objective tool to both unveil the identity of Christianity, and identify any interpretative errors. The biblical message is conveyed through the word, and the word has to be understood. To be understood, the word has to be explained. The word is rich in metaphors, which may not be taken literally. Metaphors distance one from the understanding of the second more important meaning. In order to adequately understand and discern the meaning of the metaphors used, one must apply relevant cognitive, and philosophical tools. The field of philosophy is best suited to expressing the language of reason. It can provide the indispensable theoretical concepts about what the Scriptures convey through metaphors. Greek philosophy did not initially know the Revelation of scripture. This allowed for an objective approach to look for rational means of understanding what it contained in the light of truth of the surrounding world. If the thesis seemed to contain error with reality, non-compliance with cognition, or false argumentation, it would readily be in a position to falsify it. Because philosophical systems were open to truth, which the new religion contained, it could be modified to adjust the new vision of the world, humanity, and God as Christianity introduced him. The Christian philosophy did not disturb the order of the supernatural, and the evidence was well examined prior to its acceptance. Philosophy provided the element that has historically proven to be indispensable in determining the self-consciousness of the new religion as religion, and without the help of philosophy such a vision would be incomprehensible.

In addition to Pope Benedict XVI, another Pope who may one day be renowned as a great philosopher of the twenty first century was Pope Saint John Paul II. Pope John Paul II was the second longest serving Pope in history, serving from 1978 until 2005. (Pope Pius IX served as pope for the longest period of time, serving from 1846 – 1878.) He is known as the most travelled leader in history. He was influential in improving relations between his religion, Roman Catholic, and between the other religions of Judaism, Islam, Orthodoxy, and the Anglican religions. In his opinion, Christianity through the Greek culture, was part of the providential plan of God: In his words he further supports Greek origins:

> "...in engaging great cultures for the first time, the Church cannot abandon what she has gained from her inculturation in the world of Greco-Latin thought. To

reject this heritage would be to deny the providential plan of God who guides his Church down the paths of time and history."[165]

Christianity owes much to Hellenization. Through Hellenization, Christianity was able to theoretically self-reflect, articulate its identity, and enter into an inter-religious and inter-national dialogue. Greek philosophy provided tools for intellectual self-reflection and a fair dialogue. Because of the nature of Greek Philosophy, Christianity was able to adopt the treasure of the Greek culture, yet it did not have to accept the image of the Greek world. Instead, they could reflect on the specificity of their own stance, and strongly defend their position, with other groups and nations. These groups included the Greeks and other nations; the Romans, Judaism, later with Islam, and with Para religions such as gnosis. Para religions include cults, private and invisible religions, and the non-religious esoteric belief systems that contain no supernatural beliefs. Gnosis is the Greek noun for knowledge of spiritual mysteries.

In Catholicism, there have been twelve persons given the title of Doctor of the Church. This is the title given to those recognized as contributing significantly to theology or doctrine. St. Irenaeus from Lyon was one of these figures, (about 125–202 A.D.). In his writings, he described and criticized Gnosticism and heresy, teachings that were in opposition to Christianity. Bishop Irenaeus defended the Christian perspective against the developing anti-Christian ideologies of that century.

So significant was Hellenized Christianity, that there would have been no West without it. Hellenization played a significant role in shaping the European cultural identity, as well as in building the European identity as a western one. The rejection of the Greek heritage of Christianity has the potential of significantly weakening Europe, and potentially causing the loss and destruction of centuries of tradition. The continuation of tradition allows for the survival of a civilization, namely, European civilization.

---

165 *Encyclical Letter Fides et ratio of the Supreme Pontiff John Paul II to the Bishops of the Catholic Church on the Relationship Between Faith and Reason,* VI, 72: 5 May 2018 http://w2.vatican.va/content/john-paul-ii/en/encyclicals/documents/hf_jp-ii_enc_14091998_fides-et-ratio.html.

De-Christianization of Europe in Process

The Christianity in the past, that served to unite and bond people throughout Europe, was at one time the force that identified European culture. Gradually, through three different methods, Europe became a post Christian, and then an anti–Christian culture.

Europe was united in the fifteenth century because of a common Christian belief system, giving Europe a culture of Christianity. This commonality disintegrated with the coming of the reformation, fracturing Christianity into many different denominations. The multiplicities of these Christian denominations created instability in Europe, leading to ideological and military wars.

Current European perceptions in modern times are shaped by several trends. Politics gained supremacy over religion. Both religion and the Church were eliminated from the public sphere. Europe became increasingly secularized, leading to Europe's direct opposition to Christianity, religion in general, and the Church. A new European identity began to form. Europe began to lose its traditional cultural heritage. The new identity became rooted in an anti–Christian focus.

Europe began to distance itself from Christianity. This process of the De-Christianization of Europe was not due to one factor only, but was multifaceted. Secularization was the key element. It was deeply rooted in theology, and had nothing to do with atheism. The first form of secularism brought about a belief that religion was not important. It marginalized and separated religion from other aspects of culture. Protestantism brought in a theology of human salvation that was independent of moral and religious attitudes. This belief allowed humanity to live as if one's actions had no bearing upon reaching eternal salvation. In the previous Christian (Catholic) theology, living a life directed toward reaching eternal salvation was essential. The new Christian outlook allowed people to live a life that could be led according to one's own principles and goals. Behavior had no impact on one's salvation. With Protestantism, one believed that the only requirement for salvation was a belief in Jesus Christ. Belief in God provided for a power of his grace only, independent of other factors. This perspective created a place for secularism, eliminating religion, and Christianity from public life. The impact upon public life was immense. When life is lived according to one's own whim, morality loses a focus. When there is no longer a moral code, there is an option for people to become their own God, having no need of a superior, loving, redeeming father.

Protestantism promoted a concept that behavior would not impact one's future salvation. These beliefs lead to secularism, a process whereby all public decisions, especially political ones, would be uninfluenced by religious beliefs and practices. The foundations of secularism are rooted in atheism. Atheism is an ideology that rejected the existence of God. Both practical and theoretical applications of these changes ensued. Because secularization aimed towards the total elimination of religion from both public and private lives, in reality, secularism became militant atheism. The aim of this secularism was to destroy anything connected with religion both physically and spiritually. Centres of worship were eliminated. Two significant periods of history whereby chapels and churches were eliminated, and Christian people experienced great persecution, were in the period of the French Revolution (1793), and later with the communists of the Soviet Union (The Union of the Soviet Socialist Republic, 1922). Thousands of places of worship were destroyed. The places of worship that remained were adapted for other purposes, including stores, museums, and drinking establishments.[166] Thinking had changed regarding the role of religion, which in turn changed the image of the intellectual map of Europe.

As secularism continued, the two words Christianity and church, could either be not be spoken about, could be spoken about only in a negative sense, or, could only be referred to in a historical sense. Christian Catholic philosophers who praised Europe's Christian heritage, included Edmund Burke, Georg Philipp Friedrich, and René Chateaubriand

Edmund Burke (1729–1797), Irish philosopher, politician, and author, while commenting on the events leading to the French Revolution, defended the importance of Christianity in the formation of the European identity. He postulated that the people of Europe, who were from the pre French Revolution period, experienced a unity. This unity allowed them to feel a sense of belonging anywhere in Europe. Burke attributed this unity to

---

166 Jerzy R. Nowak, *Kościół a Rewolucja Francuska [The Church and the French Revolution]*, (Szczecinek: Fundacja Nasza Przyszłość, 1999).

a variety of factors including Christianity, the tradition of the Germans and Goths, feudal institutions, and the Roman law. Much collapsed under the influence of the French Revolution, led by the fanatical and ambitions atheists (the Jacobins). France was used as the starting point for the expansion of a new universal empire.[167] The Catholic Church, the system of estates, and the universities, collapsed.

Georg Philipp Friedrich (1772–1801), otherwise known by the pen name, "Novalis", was a poet, author, mystic, and philosopher of Early German Romanticism. He enthusiastically praised the period of the middle Ages, when Europe was a Christian community living under one spiritual leader, the Pope.

Another supporter of faith was Francois – René Chateaubriand (1768–1848), a French writer, politician, diplomat, and historian. In the age when many intellectuals turned away from the church, he wrote an article entitled "In Defense of the Catholic Faith" in which he praised medieval Christianity as being genius.[168]

Anti-Christian philosophers began to play a predominant role in shaping European thought and behavior. Famous philosophers, who were clear in their anti-Christian sentiment, included Montesquieu, Voltaire, and George Grote.

Montesquieu's writings were in contrast to the thinking of the pro Christian writers and supporters. Montesquieu, also known as: Charles de Secondat, Baron de la Brede et de Montesquieu (1689–1765), advocated a government system void of religion. He was most known as a philosopher who suggested that government be divided into three branches: these were legislative, executive, and judicial systems. In his writings, he disputed the historical role of Christianity in the formation of Europe, and the importance of Christianity in its role towards building the European Identity.

---

167 Boer, *The History of the Idea*, pp. 66–7. Masonic associations with the Illuminati association at the forefront played a huge role in the eighteenth century in combating Christian tradition and culture, especially in the preparation of the French Revolution. Ulrich Im Hof, *Europa der Aufklärung* (München: Beck, 1993), pp. 219–25.

168 *The History of the Idea*, p. 69. (In French the title is "Genie du Christianisme")

He also omitted observations made more than two thousand years ago by the Greeks, who believed that Christianity had a basis of fact, and for that reason the Greeks chose to accept it. Montesquieu outlined differences between the peoples of Asia, and the peoples of Northern Europe. The peoples of Asia were slaves, and continued to be slaves, even though they were victorious in various battles. The conquered peoples were required to submit to the absolute power of their ruler. Asians needed this despotism because of the geographical conditions of the vast plains in which they lived. The Europeans were free peoples. Europeans conquered others. They maintained the integrity of freedom, offering the conquered peoples the monarchy, and freedom.[169] As the Europeans inhabited various parts of the continent, a natural shelter provided them the luxury of freedom from attack from their enemies.[170]

Voltaire (Francois – Marie Arouet 1694–1778) was a French writer and philosopher who had a negative outlook towards Christianity. According to Voltaire, the Catholic Church, and above all, the religious congregations of the Catholic Church, acted as the main hindrance to the promotion of ideas of the Enlightenment, and thus the progress of science and art.[171] The anticlericalism of Voltaire became influential and gained importance, not because of the strength and accuracy of his arguments, but rather due to the sharp language he employed.[172] For Voltaire, all Christian countries shared

---

169 Montesquieu, *On the Spirit of the Laws* (New York: The Colonial Press, 1899), I, XVII, 5: 5 May 2018 https://archive.org/details/spiritoflaws01montuoft.

170 Montesquieu, *On the Spirit* I, XVII, 6.

171 He claims that monks and nuns should be burned alive (!) in order for a faster development of science and arts. Boer, *The History of the Idea*, pp. 60–1.

172 In relation with the established image of the dark ages, first because of the Protestantism and later because of the ideology of the Enlightenment, Dawson explains the origin of this opinion and why it is superficial: "No doubt it is easy to see how the Humanist or rationalist notion of the Dark Ages arose." From the economic point of view the early Middle Ages were indeed a period of retrogression and stagnation; there were long periods of time whereby commercial activity was at a standstill and city life had almost disappeared. From the political point of view there were times in which the state was reduced almost to vanishing. Western culture preserved a spiritual energy which was independent of political power or economic prosperity. Even in the darkest periods of the Middle Ages this dynamic principle continued to operate. For what distinguishes Western culture from the other world civilizations is its

common principles of civil law, politics, and a common religious background. He thought that in Europe, the period of the Middle Ages was a time of ignorance because of the lack of freedom, the lack of rights, and the return of slavery. Changes leading to the emergence of the Enlightenment started at the end of the Middle Ages, when the Bible became secondary to science, knowledge, and learning. The history of Egypt and China became of more interest to world scholars, because of the science, knowledge, and learning, that were forthcoming from these countries.

Another philosopher, who did not believe Christianity impacted culture, was George Grote.[173] George Grote (1794 – 1871) was an English politician and historian. He believed that European identity derived from Athenian democracy and the role of the ancient Greeks, and not because of Christianity.

Some philosophers see the standpoint of George Grote as a simplification. Athenian democracy differed significantly from modern democracy, and Greek culture was multifaceted, including much more than simply politics. In defense of Christianity, it was the means by which many areas of culture were assimilated into a unique Christian European Identity.

Anti-Christian sentiments gained popularity. The role of Christianity in the formation of the European identity was negated. Anti-Christian sentiment continued to grow and flourish in Europe. The church and monarchy began to be viewed as enemies of the new concept of Europe. No longer was the will of an omnipotent God important. A death sentence was issued to Christian institutions.

---

missionary character, its transmission from one people to another in a continuous series of spiritual movements." Christianity is responsible for that. Dawson, *Religion and the Rise of Western Culture* (London: Sheed and Ward, 1950), pp. 18–9. The dark side of the Middle Ages did not stem from Christianity. It stemmed from the low level of culture of the European peoples which survived the fall of the Roman Empire. Christianity was the strength, thanks to the Europeans who did not weaken, but instead pressed forward in different areas of life.

173 Dawson observes that the secularization process was not as strong in England as in France. Dawson, *Europe and the Seven Stages*, p. 145.

Power was to originate through the will of the people[174] and was manifested through voting. Christianity was no longer the theory of the day. The new progressive Europe attempted to imitate an idea of democracy that came from the philosophy and politics of ancient Greece. The growth of ideas that favored an Anti-Christian Europe led to the French revolution (1789–1794). This time period became an epoch in history, a time chosen as the origin of an era, the reference point where time is measured. Christianity was no longer recognized as being significant in the role of a Christian identity in Europe.

Anti-Christianity and its development, was a process that was divided into several stages.[175] Methods used included: silence (one was not to speak about Christianity), negativism (Christianity could be mentioned if it was mentioned negatively), or as a historical fact. If Christianity was mentioned, it could only be referenced due to its historical significance, and not as having any relevance to modern society. Christianity was only to be considered as providing an interesting phase in history.

There was no room for Christianity in terms of a current or future perspective. Eventually Christianity was considered to be a major threat to the emerging concept of Europe. Europeanism, which was shaped by Christianity, became anti-Christian. Europe entered a post Christianity attitude.

---

174 French: *la volonté générale* it means: general or common will (the will of individuals as a group)

175 It is worth mentioning that the inventor of the word *civilization*, marquis de Mirabeau, lists religion among the factors that have the greatest influence on the civilization. His criterion which was to indicate the greatness of a civilization is moral in character. Juan R. Goberna Falque, *Civilización. Historia de una idea* (Santiago de Compostela: Univ. Santiage de Compostela, 1999), pp. 31–3. It was a paradox that the word was to be soon replaced, and thus religion was to be eliminated, and the place of morality was to be replaced by technology.

V. Europe and the Enlightenment

The new cultural age begins, the age of Enlightened Europe, or, the age of Reason. The ideology of the Enlightenment was based upon European dominance of the eighteenth and nineteenth centuries. Central beliefs included: dominance, based upon the absolute superiority of the European culture over other cultures; the unlimited power of science; the implementation of political reform on a global scale through which equality and freedom were to be realized; and lastly, upon the new paradise on Earth which was to be created.

In response to the ideology of the Enlightenment, Anti–Westernism became popular. The Occident refers to the Western World in a derogatory manner. Occident refers to the western part of the world, especially the countries of Europe and America. Anti-Occidentalism now becomes a metaphor for domestic oppression and the implementation of negative stereotypes, propagated by the enemies of the Western Continents.

The Cultural Superiority of Europe, a Myth

Did Europe have cultural superiority? How was the emerging field of science used to debate Europe's position? At one time, European culture was thought of as being superior to other cultures. This concept, during the late nineteenth century, was recognized as a myth. New fields of science began to emerge including ethnography (1834–the description of cultures), ethnology (about 1840 – the scientific explanation of the customs of individual peoples and cultures), and anthropology (late ninetieth century – the study of aspects of humans in past and present societies). These studies allowed culture to be researched using systematic analysis. The results of these studies indicated that there is no one universal civilization. Past and present cultures and civilizations may be, or may have been, superior to European civilization.

Claims that Europe was a world leader in the field of civilization and culture were dismissed. Now, cultural pluralism and cultural relativism became the ideologies of the early twentieth century. Cultural relativism believes all cultures are of equal value. Cultural pluralism allows for smaller groups within a larger society, to maintain their unique cultural identities, values and practices.

Franz Boas (1858–1942) was known for developing his theory of relativism[176], based upon his studies of race, linguistics, art, dance, and archaeology. One of his unique contributions was his study of the Inuit peoples in Baffin Island, Canada. He dispelled the myth that Western Civilization was superior to those societies that were less complex. He advocated cultural pluralism, promoting groups within societies to maintain their unique cultural identities. His criticism was directed against European domination.[177]

Science and technology grew and developed, and dominated the European influence for a time. Max Weber (1864–1920) is considered to be a founder of modern sociology. He was known to be a great supporter of the relationship between science and the European influence. He did not wish to devalue the impact of other civilizations in the formation of culture. What he did emphasize was the western contribution to the field of science. Science began to offer an orderly rational cognition. Clear scientific thought allowed for reason and a logical thinking and process.[178]

---

176 This paradigm holds that there are no absolute truths.

177 "…civilization is not something absolute, but that is relative, and that our ideas and conceptions are true only so far as our civilization goes," William H. Dall and Franz Boas, "Museums of Ethnology and their classification." *Science*, vol. 9, No. 228, 1887, p. 589. Jerry D. Moore, "Franz Boas. Culture in Context," in: *Visions of Culture. An Introduction to Anthropological Theories and Theorists*, Jerry D. More (California: AltaMira Press, 1997), pp. 33–46. Boas lived and studied in Germany, he also obtained a doctorate of psychology and later he took up geography. He emigrated to the United States (1887), where he become a professor of anthropology at the Columbia University (1899).

178 Only in the West does science exist at a stage of development which we recognize to-day as valid. Science includes but is not limited to: Empirical knowledge; reflection upon problems of the cosmos and of life; and philosophical and theological wisdom of the most profound sort. Christianity under the influence of Hellenism added more to the development of Philosophical and theological wisdom than did other cultures. Islam and a few Indian sects contributed fragments of knowledge in this area. Science utilizes knowledge and observation. India, China, Babylonia and Egypt also had greatly refined these skills towards scientific advancement. Greek contribution to the field of science

Scientific achievement has been touted as an argument in an attempt to demonstrate that other civilizations were superior to Europe. However, the contribution of science in the sphere of culture and cultural development has been misunderstood. In order for knowledge to be considered a science, that knowledge and discovery must be rooted in scientific methodology. True science contains a well defined and refined system of knowledge.

The creation of inventions came about due to a system of knowledge that was purely scientific in nature. Science itself gave rise to inventions. Some inventions were mistakenly looked at in terms of the invention itself, not the science that allowed for the invention. Science was ignored in order to argue that the culture where the invention originated was superior.

Examples of various inventions initially not known in Europe are used as a point of argument. Some of these inventions included the printing press, the compass, and the invention of paper.[179] A culture cannot be deemed superior, solely on the merit of its inventions. The scientific methodology and system of knowledge that gave rise to the invention must be considered.

---

was astounding. The study of astronomy requires a mathematical foundation which was first received from the Greeks, making Greek advancement and contribution in this area to be quite astounding. The Greek intellect promoted rational proof. Greeks created knowledge towards mechanics and physics. Greeks during the time of the renaissance added experimental methods and the modern laboratory. Greeks contributed to medicine a highly developed empirical technique, having a biological and biochemical foundation. Rational chemistry was present in the western culture.

In contrast, the study of Astronomy was lacking in Babylonia and elsewhere. Indian geometry did not focus upon a rational proof. The Indian natural sciences, though well developed in observation, lacked the experimental method. Hence medicine, especially in India, though highly developed in empirical technique, lacked a biological and particularly a biochemical foundation. A rational chemistry has been absent from all areas of culture except the West." Max Weber, *The Protestant Ethics and the Spirit of Capitalism*, trans. Talcott Parsons, (London; New York: Routledge, 2005: 5 May 2018, https://is.muni.cz/el/1423/podzim2013/SOC571E/um/_Routledge_Classics___Max_Weber-The_Protestant_Ethic_and_the_Spirit_of_Capitalism__Routledge_Classics_-Routledge__2001_pdf.

179 James Blaut M, *Eight Eurocentric Historians* (New York; London: Guilford Press, 2000), pp. 25–6.

The Europe of the Enlightenment contributed significantly to a unique concept of cognition known as scientific knowledge[180] The distinct set of concepts, theories, research methods, and standards existing in philosophy and science at this time tended to be in the fields of mathematical science, and the and fields of natural sciences. Science at this time contained a narrow paradigm that served purely utilitarian purposes. This paradigm postulated that actions were right if the majority of society found them to be useful and beneficial. The practical, useful and functional sciences of the day excluded the sciences yet to be understood or developed, including some of the social sciences. Inventions benefitting the majority, utilitarianism, were mistakenly connected with the developmental level of science. Because some inventions were not designed in the West, the contribution of Europe to the field of science was diminished.

The field of science began to evolve. The science pursued by the Enlightenment became ideologized. Now, the superiority of one science over the other became the subject of debate. Which specific model of science could be considered of higher caliber? The perceived superiority of one science paradigm over another became the vehicle to disprove the value and contribution of other science theories. Some scientific theories would be labelled unscientific. The sciences, which now became devalued, included the humanities (philosophy, metaphysics and theology), and various aspects of culture (religion and ethics).

The dispute over Europe became an ideological dispute. When the state, or when international institutions dictate the paradigm of science that is to be valid, they control the educational system, the system of research, and the system of knowledge dissemination. The concept of the Enlightenment, being considered the only valid model of science as a science, had a negative impact upon the mental understanding of Europe.

Enlightenment, mostly of the eighteenth century, was a third idea or concept of Europe. The science of the Enlightenment was a science that emphasized absolute certainty in everything that is scientific. At this time, science was expected to provide absolute trust for scientific reason. Scientific methods were questioned. Deductive reasoning studies the general, using

---

180 Latin: *theoría*.

general knowledge to make specific conclusions. Inductive science uses observation, specifically of nature, in order to learn more thoroughly about it. Inductive science studies general principles. It is a form of research that focuses upon the process of the research, and the outcome generated through its study.

Philosophers, who were expecting scientific methods to provide absolute certainty, criticized inductive science because it was not able to provide full and absolute certainty for the thesis that it presented. Using this method, exceptions would be expected to occur in either the present, or at a future time.

Karl Popper (1902–1994) criticized the inductivist method of scientific inquiry of the day. In his opinion, there was no sufficient liability connected with inductive science. According to Popper, a necessary condition existed for a scientific theory to be scientific: its hypothesis should be falsifiable. It should be able to be put to a negative test. The theory should be able to be falsified. This notion may seem as if it is a paradox. A falsifiable hypothesis is one whereby the theory could be proven wrong or false. For Popper, scientific theory must be presented in a form to be easily falsified.

The science of the Enlightenment eventually came under scrutiny. In the twentieth century, this trust in science was shaken further. Some of its premises were rejected. Premises initially thought to be valid, were not. The science of the Enlightenment lost its position in scientific circles. In social conversation, it still allows for a good conversational debate.

One belief was as follows: "It will only be a matter of time before science will enable the human person to completely master the world, and build a utopian paradise". A problem is inherent in this vision which does not fulfil the scientific criteria imposed by the Enlightenment. One cannot deduce the future in a scientific way. What is worse: the promoted paradise on Earth is becoming for millions a kind of Hell, the place of continuous tragedy. Never in the history of humanity were so many millions of people killed as was experienced in the twentieth, and in the beginning of the twenty first centuries. What made the Enlightenment project so successful was its promise to build a Paradise on Earth by means of a powerful science. Any science in the hands of immoral people can be a tool of destruction. Science itself is not a way to educate people for the good only, since education needs to have a personal dimension (the human being is a person, not an object). Science treats everything as an object. That is why a form of science that occurs without examination, analysis, or is presumed by experience[181] cannot educate people for the personal good. Only morality and religion know the way to the human person. To fulfil this task, they need to be free from the conception of science postulated through the premises and methods of the Enlightenment.

Cultural Advancement

The Greeks envisioned a democratic society based upon noble ideals. As time moved forward in history, one might wonder how noble these ideals became?

Scientific Progress and Culture

Science, and scientific knowledge, was used as a base line, to determine which culture might be the most advanced. Scientific achievement was now being used to measure cultural advancement. As time moved forward in history, the Enlightenment paradigm of science, as a science, was discredited.

Jean Jacques Rousseau's (1712–1778) political philosophy influenced, for example, the development of modern political and educational thought. He was convinced that people are good by nature, but because of society and civilization, they can become bad.

People have the tools to murder each other. Science had discovered, developed, and produced tools for destruction. The use of these tools was evidenced during the First and Second World Wars, resulting in death and victimization. The number of those affected, amounted to millions, to hundreds of millions of casualties. Science without a conscience now had become a problem on a global scale. People now have access to the tools of mass destruction, the amount of which is growing to a larger scale moment by moment in history. Science did not allow for the development of a morally based technology. Scientific knowledge had surpassed wisdom. Science had now become something that humanity would not be able to be

---

181 Latin: a priori.

proud of. If Europe wanted to lead the way in the new scientific narrative, it has reason to feel guilty.

Political Systems and Culture

Cultural advancement is measured according to the political system it employed. The political dimension of Europe only superficially referred to the Greek ideals of democracy, equality, freedom and justice. By the fourth century B.C., the system of democracy started to be viewed negatively.

Democracy was viewed as a variation of a degenerated political system similar to the systems of tyranny and oligarchy. The system of democracy itself began to change. Democracy was no longer aimed at the common good. Even though the group of citizens that would benefit from democracy may have been in the majority, democracy still aimed to benefit only a specific group of citizens. The political systems that were assessed positively were the monarchy, aristocracy, a republic, and politeia,[182] even though these systems were not considered as the absolute best political systems of the day.

When examined systemically, these systems failed. In order for a system to be effective, it needed to be adapted to the people. An ineffective system attempted to adapt the people to the system. The best system of democracy is not one that would suit all societies, in any political, economic or historical condition.

In order to determine an ideal society and the best political system, Aristotle suggested that both the historical aspect and the character of the citizens involved, needed to be considered. Not every healthy system will be the best one for each society to implement. Imposing democracy on a culture as being the only, and the best system for that society, may have negative consequences. Negative aspects of democracy include the ability of senior officials to hide harmful plans so that they are not made known to the public or minority (oligarchy). A local or international minority may also be able to exert control over the society. In this context, the democracy of

---

182 The ancient Greek word, Politeia, was used in Greek political thought, mainly by Plato and Aristotle. Later the word Politeia was used as an equivalent in the Latin republic and meant the rule of all for all.

the Enlightenment may only seemingly be part of the tradition of European Greek democracy, yet have little in common with it. As people may be unaware of the dangers connected with democracy, many may still view the European system of democracy as an ideal model of government.

Equality, Freedom, Belonging, and Culture

In a healthy system, the Greek principles of equality and freedom may be measured with reference to the common good, a levelling up. When a culture has achieved a high level, the citizens grow, giving the culture a spiritual dimension. The equality of the Enlightenment promoted mass culture. It was directed at lowering the cultural level. Democracy, which aimed to level up to the best, was replaced by a democracy, which aimed to level down to the worst. Freedom in a healthy system is concerned with the common good. It follows and applies the principle that good is allowed, and evil is not allowed. Freedom of the Enlightenment stems from liberal and individualistic factors; the most important one is freedom for selfishness. The common good does not limit freedom. Freedom is limited by the egoism of other citizens. The freedom of the other is the limit of my freedom. In practice, the freedom of the Enlightenment led to unlimited power of a bureaucratic state. Through an excess of positive law, it was able to reduce the real freedom of its citizens to the minimum. Freedom for the common good, in a relativistic society, neglects freedom for the minority. In Nazi Germany, some people had unlimited "freedom" to persecute others. The same may be said for Rwanda and other parts of the world that have experienced genocide. The equality of democracy may mask various forms of inequality. The one, who has power, especially the power of money, the media, or political power, may be the driving force towards current laws and practices of the society.

Finally, the universal goal of belonging that the Enlightenment was meant to generate was not universal. It applied only to those who accepted its principles. Those who did not accept the principles of the Enlightenment were excluded or discriminated against. The banner of the French Revolution read: Liberty, Equality, Fraternity, or Death.[183]

---

183 (*ou la mort*): Vendee was an example of planned state's extermination of Catholic population only because they were Catholics. In the course of

Society's Role in Cultural Advancement

For the Greeks, society existed for several purposes. One ideal of the Greek culture included the desire to provide for a mutual provision of service. Another purpose was to fulfil the basic human desire to be together. Being together is based upon an innocent friendship that is not self-seeking. Society for the Greeks was also about existing for a higher purpose. Social life is an opportunity for people to treat each other nobly and beautifully. The Greek word kalokagathía may be referenced to imply virtuous conduct.[184] In a healthy system, a citizen would not threaten another citizen, especially with the threat of death.

The civilization of the Enlightenment initially aimed to create a paradise on earth. A change of this noble goal originated during the French Revolution. Mass murders were committed, serving as a tangible sign of a bleak future. The civilization initially dreamed of, instead has been turned into a culture of death.

---

18 months approximately 120 thousand people were killed, that is 15 % of the population. Murders were cruel and ruthless, e.g. pheasants and priests were loaded onto ships to sink them in the middle of the river. Reynald Secher, *Le Génocide franco-français–La Vendée-Vengé* (Paris: Presses Universitaires de France, 1986).

184 Aristotle, *Politics*, V, 14.

VI. Europe, Political Systems, and the European Union

How did the concept of a united Europe start, what was its purpose? From an historical perspective, European clashes encompass much of Europe's history. The clash between the Persians and the Greeks was the first concept.[185] The clash between the Christians and the Muslims became a second concept. Then the clash within Christianity itself became a concept of Europe. All these clashes defined Europe as a culture.

The current concept of Europe is becoming the European Union, also called the E.U., or, the Union. This concept is complex, variable, and not fully fixed. The Union is in the process of changing, and being modified according to the current balance of political forces in the Europe that exists in the moment. The final status or condition that the European Union will become cannot as yet be determined. Of note, it recently has taken a stance in opposition to its original objectives and goals.

Europe, as it pertains to several different concepts, is of the old school of thought. It is attempting to create one, unified member state. The first attempt to create a single European Member state is attributed to Charlemagne. Charlemagne was the king of the Franks[186], and the first emperor of the Holy Roman Empire. He is especially remembered for his advocacy of education.

In more recent times, a pressing need again arose to create a united Europe. The context of uniting Europe under the European Union came from a desire to prevent another war such as was experienced through the

---

185 The Achaemenid Dynasty, the first Persian Empire, was located in Western Asia, and existed for two centuries, between 550–330 B.C. It was a monarchy founded by Cyrus the Great. The "Perses" attempted to conquer Greece, but, instead, they were conquered by Alexander the Great between 334 and 327 B.C.

186 The Franks were German speaking peoples who invaded the western Roman Empire in the fifth Century. The Franks controlled a large area of early medieval western Europe, including what is now northern France, Belgium, and western Germany. They established a strong Christian kingdom.

Second World War (1939–1945). This global war began in Europe. It caused unimaginable material damage and loss of life. More than seventy million people were killed during this war. Following the war, Europe became marginalized on a global scale. Europe became powerless and unimportant. A future war of this nature would most probably destroy Europe.[187] Prevention of another similar war became paramount in people's minds.

Political unity was undertaken among government agencies with the purpose of creating and maintaining a peaceful Europe for the future. This required international cooperation among European countries.

Economics and Europe

Initiatives were developed in Europe to maintain its internal and external stability following the Second World War crisis. A global cooperation initiative was established. Europe organized itself together to form a united Europe focusing upon ethical aims. Objectives included: The prevention of a single military power that could obtain dominance over another; and to increase prosperity through the linking of economies.

The first aim was to prevent military power. The global initiative cooperated in order to prevent any country, especially Germany, from the independent growth of industrial power. Industrial power is the basis of contemporary military power. Without this independent, high level of industry in the area of military power, waging and winning a war becomes impossible.

The linking of economies was established as the second proposal, to instill cooperation instead of competitiveness. Germany and France next led an initiative to link the economies of several major European countries.[188]

---

187 As Karl Jaspers noted: "Europe was large and became small" ("Europa ist klein geworden"). Jaime F. Barrio, „Europa en el pensamiento de Jaspers," *Pensamiento. Revista de investigación e información filosófica*, Vol. 53, No. 205 (1997), p. 91.

188 A broad aim of economic linking was presented as follows: "The solidarity in production thus established will make it plain that any war between France and Germany becomes not merely unthinkable, but materially impossible. The setting up of this powerful productive unit, open to all countries willing to take part, will ultimately bind all the member countries, and provide them with the basic elements of industrial production on the same terms, and will lay a

The first organizational form of the uniting of countries was called the European Coal and Steel Community (1952). Then, a few years later the European Economic Community (1958) was formed. A growing number of countries decided to join this community to protect Western Europe against an internal war; to provide for the development of industry, trade, and entrepreneurship; and to increase prosperity.

Europe in the 1950's and 1960's, had found a reason to be optimistic within the post-war concept of Europe. Europe had achieved a broad level of economic cooperation and development.

Ideology and Europe

Each independent European country had its own way of viewing political leadership and ideologies. Democracy, Nazism, fascism, and communism, each influenced the future direction of Europe prior to the Second World War.

In order to prevent another, or a Third World War in Europe, it was hoped that a united economic system would eliminate that possibility. The economy has a direct influence on social life in its various forms, but the economy is not an end in itself. The economy is usually based on some ideology, which defines immediate and future targets for different dimensions of social life. These targets may lead to either co-operation or war. It therefore became necessary to diagnose threats that stem from ideology. With regard to the Second World War, three ideologies posed a threat to Europe: Nazism, fascism and communism. Nazism prevailed in the Third Reich, Fascism in Italy, and Communism in the Soviet Union.

Nazism

Wars in the nineteenth century stemmed from the growth of European nationalisms. Forms of nationalism were emerging in England, France, and Russia. The nationalisms in these countries were used as an attempt to refer to the concept of the chosen people described in the Old Testament.

---

true foundation for their economic unification." *The Schuman Declaration, 9 May 1950,* http://europa.eu/about-eu/basic-information/symbols/europe-day/schuman-declaration/index_en.htm.

National Socialism, *Nazionalsozialismus*, abbreviated as Nazism, referred to the nationalism of the German nation. Germany based its nationalism on science, or rather in pseudo-science, by basing its principles upon racism.[189]

The German nation in the pre Second World War period operated under two premises: firstly, that the German nation, the Aryan race, was superior to all other nations and peoples of the world; its second premise was socialism. The practice of socialism gave Germany a defined organizational framework. Socialism aimed to ensure that carried out actions were effective, and optimal for the German nation. The belief in a superior Aryan race, combined with a practice of socialism, propagated the total primacy of the society (state) over an individual, and allowed for Germany to justify their right to rule over other nations and eventually the whole world. These ideologies allowed for the creation of such a powerful German State, that Germany was able to wage the war upon the world for nearly six years.

The Third Reich nationalism, (Nazism), can be criticized on many different levels. From both the theoretical and humanistic point of view, these ideologies lacked scientific basis.[190] The racism as portrayed through Nazism, rejected human dignity in relation to the non-German nations and non-Aryan races, and as a result legitimizes violence, wars, war crimes, and murder.

Following the Second World War, the strongest opposition to Nazism and racism was expressed in the Universal Declaration of Human Rights (1948). This declaration was written in response to the atrocities of the Second World War committed by those in Germany who were able to rise to power, and subdue the rest of the German nation, into submission. This declaration was to serve as a model for future human worldwide conduct, hopefully preventing similar future wars based upon racist and socialist actions. This declaration stated the following: "Disregard and contempt

---

189 Erwin Baur, Eugen Fischer, Fritz Lenz, *Grundriss der menschlichen Erblichkeitslehre und Rassenhygiene*, (München: J. F. Lehmanns Verlag, 1921), Vol. 1–2 5 May 2018 https://archive.org/details/grundrissdermens02bauruoft.

190 Piotr Jaroszyński, *Człowiek i nauka. Studium z filozofii kultury* [Man and Science. Studies in the Philosophy of Culture] (Lublin: Polskie Towarzystwo Tomasza z Akwinu, 2008), pp. 283–7.

for human rights have resulted in barbarous acts which have outraged the conscience of mankind" (Preamble).[191]

Those barbarous acts were murders committed on an unprecedented scale during the Second World War. Murders were justified by those who committed them, because of their unwarranted belief in the superiority of one nation over another. The Universal Declaration of Human Rights clearly stated that: "Recognition of the inherent dignity and of the equal and inalienable rights of all members of the human family is the foundation of freedom, justice and peace in the world" (Preamble[192])

Dignity, in this declaration of rights, is considered to exist both on the anthropological level and as a consequence in law. As an anthropological category, the word dignity indicates a basic and inalienable equality and autonomy of all people.

Fascism

Fascism originated in Italy. It was developed to reflect the ideology of the Italian State. The word fascism is derived from the Latin word fasces, meaning a bundle of rods, worn by a clerk, or lector. This bundle was highly symbolic of the unity and strength inherent when a single rod was joined into to a bundle. Fascism operated under two initial values, despotism (a government ruling with absolute power), and totalitarianism (complete governmental authority over every aspect of private and public life). Through these two values, the state would guarantee unity. The inherent values of Totalitarianism and Fascism became linked and synonymous.[193]

---

191 Julia Jaskólska, "Powody i okoliczności proklamowania Powszechnej Deklaracji Praw Człowieka [Reasons and Circumstances of Proclaiming the Universal Declaration of Human Rights]," *Człowiek w kulturze* [Man in Culture], Vol. 11 (1998), pp. 27–48.

192 *Universal Declaration of Human Rights*: 5 May 2018 http://www.un.org/en/universal-declaration-human-rights/

193 Paweł Tarasiewicz, "Jan Paweł II o totalitaryzmie" [John Paul II on Totalitarianism], in: *Totalitaryzm: jawny czy ukryty?* [Totalitarianism: Open or Hidden?] (Lublin: Lubelska Szkoła Filozofii Chrześcijańskiej), 2011, pp. 223–4.

The word "totalitarianism" originated in Italy during a speech delivered by Benito Mussolini in which he outlined the beliefs and aims guiding future actions of the state: "For the Fascist, everything is in the State, and nothing human or spiritual exists, much less has value – outside the State."[194]

The word totalitarian originated in the speech, understood and implied, through its Italian definition of the word. The equivalent word in English is everything. "Tutto" is from an Italian word, and "totum" is from the Latin word signifying all or everything. Since in this kind of a state everything (totum) is for a state, this kind of state started to be called totalitarian.[195]

Fascism initially was created for Italy and Italy alone. It did not aspire to become a universal ideology to be imposed on all countries, nor meant to be implemented on a global scale as communism was. Because it embodied both right and left wing ideologies, it has been classified as being extreme in both directions. Fascism in itself contained positive aspects to its ideology. From the historical and social point of view it expressed the idea that successful people do not act in isolation, but are united like fasces (the bound bundle of rods). Individual action is weak. The word Fascism in itself and its historical meaning was not negative. It was the intention of propagandists, to impose on this word a false and (pejorative) derogatory meaning. The action of propaganda was effective. The negative meaning for the word Fascism was later accepted by the uneducated mob. The Soviets during the Second World War referred to their opponents as fascists. Later, when the war ended, the Allies also referred to fascism negatively, as being solely a right-wing extremist ideology. The concept of Fascism took on a derogatory connotation largely due to propaganda.

The ideology of fascism was rejected after the defeat of Italy in the war.[196] Fascism now only exists as an historical and political category, mainly used

---

194 Mussolini, *Dottrina del fascismo*, 1932, in: Paul O'Brien, *Mussolini in the First World War. The Journalist, the Soldier, the Fascist* (Oxford; New York: Berg, 2005), p. 1.

195 "La nostra formula é questa: tutto nello stato, niente al di fuori dello stato, nulla contro lo stato," Norberto Bobbio, *Dal fascismo alla democrazia. I regimi, le ideologie, le figure, e le culture politiche* (Milano: Baldini & Castoldi, 2008), p. 51.

196 Peter F. Sugar, "Fascism and Nationalism," in: *Encyclopedia of Nationalism* (San Diego;San Francisco: Academic Press, 2001), pp. 285–7.

for academic purposes.[197] Fascism, as a totalitarianism ideology, recognized the total primacy of the state over the individual, and thereby threatened human rights. When Italy was defeated, Italy adopted the ideology of the Allies. Fascism fell.

It was not the fascism of the past in Italy that posed a threat when creating the future European Union. The future threat originated from the Soviet Union, and the ideology that the country of Russia embraced, the ideology of Communism.

Communism

Russia played a significant role in the changing ideologies and power structures of Europe, beginning with the Russian revolution in 1905. The Russian Revolution may have led to the February Revolution of 1917, whereby royalty (the Czar) resigned, and a provisional government was created. Soon after, a civil war broke out. During the historic October revolution, the Bolsheviks (a strong military and political group) gained power through a coup d'état (a quick and decisive seizure of governmental power). The Bolsheviks did not have a majority government. The Bolshevik leader, Lenin, ruled from a position of the majority. He invented the name 'bolshevique', a term that he believed (successfully) would make an impression on the people. Russia became the Union of the Soviet Socialist Republic (USSR). The official name Soviet Union was adopted in 1922. In 1918 the Soviet Union withdrew from the First World War, giving up much of its land and resources. The Bolsheviks introduced communism in Russia by

---

197 This is one of broader academic definitions of fascism: „... fascism may be defined as a form of revolutionary, ultra-nationalism, that is designed for national rebirth. It is based primarily on vitalism as a philosophy. It is structured on extreme elitism, mass mobilization, and the *Führerprinzip*. It positively values violence as an end as well as the means, and tends to normalize war and/or military virtues," *Encyclopedia*, pp. 286–7. Vitalism is a school of scientific thought attempting to explain the nature of life. Fuhrerprinzip is an ideology whereby organizations are made up of a hierarchy of leaders. Each leader has absolute responsibility in a specific area and answers only to the leader's superiors. The leader requires absolute obedience from subordinates.

force. The intent of the Bolsheviks was to conquer Europe first, and then the world.

Poland was able, in 1920, to successfully prevent being conquered by Russia, and prevented Russia from expanding into its borders. This resistance was not successful in 1939. Both Russia and Germany desired the conquest of Poland. Poland became the first act of aggression between Russia and the third Reich of Germany. On September 1st, 1939, Poland was invaded by Germany, and on September 17th, 1939, Poland was invaded by the Soviets. In the agreement of August 23rd, 1939, between Russia and the third Reich, Poland was divided between them.

World tensions continued to rise. The Second World War began on September 1, 1939. Later, Germany invaded the USSR in June of 1941. The threat of Soviet Communism against the West continued. However, ideological issues, including the communist agenda, were pushed into the background between Russia and other nations. Russia and the West united in their war efforts against Germany. Nazism became the greater threat to Europe. A war raged in Europe against a common enemy: German Nazism. The countries were in an external war.

Internally within both the communist country of Russia, and the Nazi society of Germany, both raged an internal war. This war was in the form of persecution against people of faith. Christians and Jews were especially targeted. Both societies, because of their atheistic premise, were against any religion.

During the Second World War, the communist state's main objective was to manage and subdue the threat from Nazi Germany. Although persecution within Russia continued, Stalin during this time period was friendlier towards the Orthodox Church than the Roman Catholic one. Following the war, persecution of non-atheists increased in Russia. Following the war, ideological arguments returned between nations, and new political make-ups emerged.

New Political Change

The Second World War ended. Europe was divided; beliefs and convictions from different world powers became polarized. The Second World War officially ended with the surrender of the third Reich in 1945. German Nazism and the third Reich of Germany, no longer threatened Europe, it no longer existed. In 1947, the exact details of peace were formulated and expressed with the Paris Peace Treaty, mainly agreed upon between the West and the Soviet Union. The problem: Europe was split up between two opposing and emerging systems, the capitalist, and the communist. The capitalist system included the western part of Germany and other countries including France, the Netherlands (Holland), and Italy. The Communist Bloc included the Eastern part of Germany, and countries including Czechoslovakia, Poland, and Romania. The Communist Bloc controlled by Moscow became the new emerging threat to the West, stemming from their ideological differences.

The concept of one Europe emerged, the European Union. Proponents hoped all countries could be included in this one Europe, including those that were within the borders of the Soviet Bloc.

The concept of a European Union was not new. It was first formulated in the face of the threat of Nazi ideology from Germany, and later due to the Soviet threat of communism. Following the Second World War, Nazi ideology was denounced and the party dissolved, no longer threatening Europe. The economy of West Germany was included into the mechanisms of the international economy of the west.

Following the Second World War, Communism became the new threat to peace. The ideology and the official doctrine of the Soviet Union and its satellites, took the form of propaganda, and political and military offence.[198] Another war loomed over Europe.

Christian-Democratic Movement, the European Union

Europe now has a society under a European Union. How and for what purposes was this Union created? Does the Union represent a positive influence towards the future of Europe and its culture? We are left with questions.

---

198 It was an opportunity to stop the process of de-Nazification in Germany, i.e. to stop the processes against the war-criminals. Wiesław Bokajło, *Koncepcja Europy Konrada Adenauera i jej realizacja w praktyce politycznej w latach 1945–1954* [The Idea of Europe According to Konrad Adenauer and its Realization in Political Practice in the Years 1945–1954] (Wrocław: Wydawnictwo Uniwersytetu Wrocławskiego, 1995), p. 99.

Europe was devastated following the Second World War. The threat of a third war loomed, due to hostilities, which again began to rise. Christian leaders struggled to divert such a disaster through joint efforts and a united proposal. A united Europe, joined together towards health and prosperity, became the strategy of Christian leaders. Many obstacles needed to be identified and overcome in order for this hope to become a reality.

Europe began a process of de-Christianization that began during the Enlightenment. This process was not continuous. During the difficult moments of history, world events brought the merits of Christianity back into favor. The two world wars had tragic consequences for humanity, and outraged Europeans consciences. Communities embracing Christian ideals re-entered the public arena in a very significant way.

Christian groups developed an action plan that was based upon their beliefs about maintaining peaceful human relationships, respect, and value for all human life. These groups began to look towards a common purpose in maintaining world peace. Christian democracy was organized in the institutional form of a political party.

Don Luigi Sturzo was an Italian Roman Catholic priest and politician. He was the secretary general of Catholic Action. He was a political organizer, who, in 1915, founded the Christian democratic concept of European integration, and the Italian Popular Party (Partito Popolare Italiano – PPI). In the early 1920's, he proposed an economic and political Union of the European states, in the form of the Common Market.

At the end of the Second World War, Germany no longer threatened Europe. Now the Soviets were to be feared. Both politicians and religious leaders were concerned. General de Gaulle in his memoirs cited Pope Pius XII, as saying: "Averting the danger of extension of the Soviet Union's influence to Western Europe, can only be achieved through close cooperation between states guided by Catholicism – Germany, France, Italy, Spain, Belgium and Portugal."[199]

Catholicism in this context may be understood to refer to the Christian values of charity, respect, equality, and universal humanistic values, that the three Catholic politicians, Schuman, Adenauer, and Gasperi, embraced

---

[199] Bokajło, *Koncepcja Europy*, pp. 15–6.

when attempting to find peaceful solutions to an agitated Europe. The formation of a common Union continued to seem attractive in diverting hostilities. In the political arena, three already mentioned Catholic democratic politicians are considered to be the founding fathers of the European Union. In Western Europe Christian principles formed the basis for building a united Europe.

Christian values significantly influenced Europe in the social shaping of civilization, and in politics. Every person in the world was valued. This belief stemmed from the universal law of love and charity, which makes all people our neighbor.[200] Science, education, hospitals, and the social welfare of feeding and caring for the poor, were all developed with Christian values in mind. The dignity of work became appreciated. Robert Schuman (1886–1963), was a prime minister of France and a Christian Democrat (M.R.P.). He was one of the founders of the European Union, the Council of Europe, and NATO. He wrote: "Christianity taught about the inherent

---

200 "Jacques Maritain, our great Christian philosopher, that we French made the mistake of sending to a far-off university instead of ourselves profiting from his seminal teaching, has remarked on this parallelism of development between the Christian idea and democracy. Christianity teaches equality of the nature of all men, children of the same God, redeemed by the same Christ, without distinction of race, color, class or profession. It identified the dignity of work and the duty of us all to comply with it. It recognized the primacy of spiritual values, which are the sole to ennoble man. The *universal law of love and charity made each man our neighbor* and on this is built social relations in the Christian world. All this teaching and the practical consequences which devolve from it have *changed the world*. This revolution took place under the progressive inspiration of the Gospel which fashioned the generations slowly, and sometimes accompanied with it painful struggles. In fact, the progress of civilization has neither been automatic nor in one direction only: recollections of the past and base instincts of a repugnant nature have weighed on this development and continue to oppose it. If that is true for those of us who are privileged, and who have been Christians for generations, how much is it applicable to those who have just had their first contacts with Christianity." *Robert Schuman on Democracy*: 11 May 2018 http://users.belgacombusiness. net/schuman/democracy.htm. Similarly, de Gasperi referring to Henri Bergson, believed that democracy is evangelical in nature and love is its driving force, *I fondatori*, p. 177.

equality of all human beings, children of the same God, redeemed by the same Christ, regardless of race, skin color, class and profession."[201]

The basis of democracy, in a deeper sense, and the formation of European culture, originated from Christianity. It was not purely political. Democracy may be traced back to anthropological roots, where the belief in the equality of all people, in the context of human dignity, emerged as a category in itself. One aspires to learn from the experience of the past. In this context, neither economy nor politics can be treated as an end in itself. Economy and politics must both serve the spiritual dimension of human life.[202]

This belief system only appeared with the beginning of Christianity. It is important again to refer to Christian thinking in the context of the development of democracy. In the Christian perspective, the human being was created in the likeness and image of a supreme and loving God.[203] Christians had an influence because of their striving to follow the Ten Commandments and the Beatitudes, directing the behavior of a person toward the good of others before self-interest.

Political and economic decisions were now made independently from church and religion.[204] Because politicians, during this time period, were Christian, Christian ideals and spiritual foundations were incorporated into political and economic decisions. For example: After the Second World War, the original concept of one Europe, was put into practice.

Alcide De Gasperi (1881–1954) was an Italian prime minister who was one of the founders of both the Christian Democratic Party and the

201 Robert Schuman, *Pour l'Europe* (Paris: Éditions Nagel, 1964), p. 57.

202 Anneliese Poppinga, "O osobowości Konrada Adenauera. Polityk i chrześcijanin" [On the Personality of Konrad Adenauer. A Politician and a Christian], in: *Konrad Adenauer. Europa chrześcijańska. Christliches Europa*, Documentation of Polish and German scientific on 15th and 16th December 1994 (Lublin: Towarzystwo Naukowe Katolickiego Uniwersytetu Lubelskiego: Fundacja Rozwoju KUL, 1995), p. 56.

203 "A person has a unique dignity given by God and the value of each individual is irreplaceable," Konrad Adenauer *Staatsauffasung*, Bonn 7.04.1946: 7 May 2018, https://www.konrad-adenauer.de/biographie/zitate/staatsauffassung.

204 *I fondatori del Europa Unita secondo il progetto di Jean Monnet, Robert Schuman, Konrad Adenauer, Alcide de Gasperi* (Cantalupa: Effatà Editrice 1999), pp. 194–6.

European Union. De Gasperi described Europe based upon the strength of feelings, a concept capable of stimulating consciousness and will.[205] The original Union made decisions that focused upon morality, human dignity, and human fraternity. The decisions that were part of the original Union, stem from Christian values and teachings, and from the cultural and spiritual heritage of a common civilization which originated from Christianity.[206]

Creating a United Europe

A European Union became a reality. The initial goals and objectives of the Union became displaced. In attempting to build a system of European unity through the creation of the European Union, there were a multitude of inherent problems. These problems existed within and between the states, and the nations. Among the people, problems included: a lack of trust and good will towards honest cooperation; a history of a Europe that had experienced many conflicts and wars; differing religions; interests; and belief systems; different aspirations and hopes towards the future society; and different self-evaluations. Value differences included honesty and faith; education and science; and tradition and customs. The most significant value difference involved force and leadership. All of these issues were more significant than economic barriers.

The founding fathers of the European Union were well aware of the many problems that could arise in creating a united Europe. They still believed a united Europe would be essential if Europe were to continue to be a Europe in the future. Without unity, Europe was destined to collapse. Confrontations stemming from differing convictions of involved world powers, especially the threat of communism, could only escalate. Cooperation was a necessity for Europe. The era of small and independent states was gone. Saving the historical identity of the European nations became the most important factor when working towards a united Europe.

A clear idea of cooperation was now of paramount importance in overcoming the challenges of forming a united Europe. Four major strategies were formulated. The first was to demonstrate the common deeper European

---

205 I fondatori, pp. 207–8.
206 I fondatori, pp. 207–8.

roots (historical and axiological) of the values that built a European identity, stemming from the Greek, Roman, and Christian histories. The second strategy was to demonstrate the common danger and evil that communism would create. The third was to look for common values for a peaceful future. The fourth strategy was to create clear rules and guidelines for future cooperation and justice. This cooperation would need to be formalized and institutionalized in order to be effective, cooperation based upon common values and ends for all. Without proper axiology (attention to values and value judgments), it would only be a matter of time before the economy would collapse.

Konrad Adenauer (1876–1967) was in charge of the Christian Democratic Party of the German Government following World War 11. Through his leadership, Germany moved from devastation to prosperity and economic stability, achieving democracy. He promoted common Christian values as a means of uniting Europe. The largest threats to these values were liberalism, materialism, and the expansion of communism as practiced by the Soviet Union.[207] Both materialism and liberalism were equally hostile to the values of the Christian people, who advocate strong family and social life. Historically, materialism and liberalism played a destructive role in Germany due to their negative impact on both family and social life.[208]

Christian theologians warned against de Christianizing society. A Christian society focuses upon the meaning and purpose of human life, which is beyond the range of the normal physical human experience, fulfilled in the transcendent dimension. Economy or politics do not create cultural values by themselves, because they are focused only on the means, and not the end. The ideals and values that led Christian leaders towards a united Europe lost their focus.

Adenauer and Schuman were two influential Christian intellectuals. Konrad Adenauer was a strong promoter of the value of a Christian nation in terms of stability. According to Adenauer: the de-Christianization

---

207 Hanns Jürgen Küsters, "Konrad Adenauer – polityka integracyjna i antykomunizm" [*Political Integration and Anticommunism*], in: *Konrad Adenauer. Europa chrześcijańska*, p. 110.

208 Küsters, "Konrad Adenauer," p. 116.

and the collapse of spiritual culture pose a threat to Europe.[209] In 1952 Adenauer stated that Europe could be either Christian or pagan, but not both. He warned that the godless communism of the Soviet Union, and all left-winged parties, would lead Europe in the latter direction.[210] The final result will be nihilism and hopelessness.[211]

Robert Schuman also warned against anti-Christian doctrine. For him, legislation must not violate and exceed the Divine law.[212] In formulating a united Europe, he believed that the Christianity that had been operational for nearly two thousand years should continue.[213] Promoting Christianity was especially needed in terms of ethical standards in public life. The achievements and contributions of Christianity to culture could not be ignored in generating a future peaceful Europe.

It becomes prudent to examine the projects of the current European Union of the twenty first century. Projects have moved in the alternate direction, a direction that is not Christian in terms of values or practice. The policies of the Union have moved towards that of paganism, utopia, and materialism. Projects involve such highly organized schemes of per-fection that they are impossible to achieve. Other projects focus upon the acquisition of material goods. The concept of a loving God is treated with contempt. Denied is the prospect of salvation, where it is possible to live a life after death with a loving God, or alternatively, it is possible to live a life of hell and damnation, based upon the decisions and the life a person chooses while living on this earth.

---

209 "Great technical progress is being made but I wonder: what about the spiri-tual progress? Is the spirit of a "MAN" keeping up with those extraordinary changes? Is the "MAN" becoming a slave of technology, a slave of what he has created himself? Poor humanity launches rockets to the Moon but forgets about the richness of culture, about its threats and above all how difficult it is to create a true culture – how easy it is to destroy it and how hard it is to build it again" *I fondatori*, p. 133. "The future of West in the long term is threatened primarily not by political tension but by the massification, unifica-tion of thought and feelings, shortly speaking – whole way of life, escape from responsibility, thinking only about oneself (1952), *I fondatiori*, p. 133.

210 *I fondatori*, p. 118.

211 Poppinga, "O osobowości" [On Personality], in: *Konrad Adenauer* p. 53.

212 Wahl, *Robert Schuman. Ojciec Europy* [Father of Europe], p. 82.

213 Wahl, *Robert Schuman. Ojciec Europy* [Father of Europe], p. 117.

Christians complain that materialism has taken on its own doctrine, aiming to deprive a person of the opportunity and right to a spiritual life, and a future hope of achieving a joy that comes from an eternity in paradise with a supreme God. A person's purpose to live becomes shallow, focusing upon the world, the here and now, and the state. This view, according to Christians, sets a precedent upon a dangerous set of rules and theories whose aim is to deprive Europe of its spiritual dimension. A culture making human genius possible through the historical roots of the revelation of a supreme God becomes inaccessible.

VII. The European Union Rejects Christianity

What does it mean to be a Christian in the world of the European Union? There are many implications. Moving forward towards creating a united Europe, treaties were, and will continue to be signed, developed and agreed to. What is significant is the continued de-Christianization of Europe, as noted when the treaties are examined in succession from the first to the most recent.

Treaties and the Developing European Union

Treaties to examine in succession of their origin, include: The European Economic Community (EEC – 1957, or the Common Market); The Maastricht Treaty (1992); The Amsterdam Treaty (1997); The Charter of Fundamental Rights (2000–2009); The Convention of the Council of Europe (May 2001); Treaty of Nice (2000–2001); and The Treaty establishing a Constitution for Europe (2004).

As the European culture historically was developed because of Christianity, and as the European Union was developed to promote peace and prosperity specifically based upon Christian principles, these treaties will be examined with specific reference to their anti-Christian stance.

The European Economic Community (EEC – 1957), also known as the Common Market, was first in Europe's movement towards economic and political Union, paving the way for a new stage of European integration.

Later the Maastricht Treaty (1992) transformed this Community into the European Union. To date twenty-eight-member states are included. Through this treaty, a European citizenship was created. Also included were common foreign policies; a means towards future European integration; and foundations for the developing and implementing a common currency. This currency has been named the Euro, a word shortened from the word European. The Treaty was signed with a view towards strengthening economic and political relations between the Member States, in order to give the Union the status of a state, with all the attributes, in which a state is entitled to. The document contained many valuable categories, including freedom; democracy; respect for human rights; history; culture; and traditions.[214]

What is interesting and what is a significant, is the total removal and elimination of God, Christianity, and religion from this document.[215] A deliberate separation had now been made between the concept of Europe within the European Union, and Christianity. The document was not based upon, nor did it make any reference to theory, philosophy, doctrine, beliefs, or ideas that support a human foundation for peace, love and forgiveness, or forming the deeper foundations of the human spirit. Without reference to deeper foundations, the document deprives humanity of good moral teachings, becoming demagogic and hollow.

The Amsterdam Treaty (1997) replaced the Maastricht Treaty. Powers from national governments were transferred to the European Parliament. This treaty included policies on immigration, civil and criminal laws, foreign policy, and changes allowing for new member nations to join the E.U. The Treaty of Nice (2000–2001) was designed to address Eastern expansion of the European Union. Words not included in these documents were God, Christianity, and religion.

The Charter of Fundamental Rights was developed in 2000, signed after some modifications in Lisbon in 2007 and entered into force in 2009. This charter addressed fundamental human rights protected in the E.U., including dignity, freedoms, equality, solidarity, citizens' rights, justice, and civic duties. Although Christian values were addressed, the source of these values was not present. The Treaty establishing a Constitution for Europe (2004) also did not contain any mention of God or Christianity. This charter contained a brief mention of spiritual, religious and moral heritage but it is not known which specific heritage that the document referred to.[216]

---

214 Preamble.
215 Latin: signum temporis. A sign of the times.
216 Preamble.

The Impact of Changing Values upon Society

The influence of the anti – Christianity era begins to affect cultural change. The development of this new culture of Europe is based upon the rejection of the Greek and Christian heritage, and the heritage of the Enlightenment. All elements of the previous European identity are lost, one following the other. New ideas are introduced, with devastating results. Europe ceases to be categorized as a civilization.

The initial impetus towards a united Europe, was based upon the values of a society that welcomes Christianity in their midst. Christian Democratic communities, and Christian dominion, had a great impact upon bringing stability to a war-torn Europe. The practice of Christianity, for the Christian people, will continue to be threatened in Europe through the developing treaties. These treaties gradually not only neglect to include Christian fundamental values, but they gradually eliminate, and then fundamentally reject these values.

The ideology of the Enlightenment casts a shadow over Europe. Other civilizations, such as the African or Asian civilizations, currently may perceive Europe as a degenerated civilization, from which you can only gain material prosperity.

The current civilization of Europe, (and many other countries who follow similar ideologies), may be viewed as one that is doomed to have no future. Philosophically speaking, faith and the family are two foundations for the development of civilization. If these two foundations are undermined, society in subsequent generations will shrink in its achievements. One advantage, that Christianity and Christian practices offers, is the promotion of the foundations of faith and family. When these foundations are eliminated, heritage and land will be taken over by communities from other civilizations. The price that Europe will pay for abandoning the principles and ideals that Christianity offers, is increasing.

Under the European Union, Christianity is being abandoned for the ideals of secularism.

Those who do not share the Christian world view may find some parts of the next section to be disturbing. Some readers may strongly oppose some topics as they are presented. The secular world view and the Christian world view are in some aspects in opposition. A thorough understanding of each divergent perspective may assist in working towards achieving common ground in philosophical debates, particularly when they involve such controversial topics in our current society.

The Union advocates a process of abandoning the principles connected with the religion of Christianity, and, in some situations, demonstrates hostility towards Christian ideals. Christianity is becoming unpopular as a worldview. Christians, when they attempt to debate laws or standards of society contrary to those stemming from Christian values, are called racist and bigoted. Christians in some situations may be viewed negatively, minimally tolerated, and in some situations directly persecuted. Some may postulate that the current society is more advanced on the road to socialism, than was Eastern Europe during the period of communism.

Christianity advocates that the foundations of faith and the family be preserved. Secularism believes in living for the moment, a happiness that is based upon personal desires, having little respect or belief in a future beyond this current life. When no God exists outside of oneself, the self becomes the god to be worshipped. Christianity promotes a style of life that is concerned with a higher purpose, a thinking that suggests that life may not end at the moment of human death, and that a person not willing to seek the mercy of God, will be required to face that same God's justice.[217]

Christians currently live more and more as a minority (except in Poland) in a democratic society that seeks to follow a majority secular viewpoint. This secular majority aims to silence the minority that advocates a movement toward a goal with a higher purpose. Instead, the secular majority promotes a culture that does not value life. The Self versus the Other, and Self Gratification, are promoted by the secular majority as the primary motive for human existence.

---

217 Father Chris Alar in his video presentation Entitled "Divine Mercy 101", discusses what he believes to be a Christian responsibility to vocalize Christian concepts, in spite of the negative labels attributed to Christians for doing so. The "spiritual works of Mercy" involve "teaching the ignorant" and "correcting sinners". He states Christians "must be vocal about those things that are contrary to the will of God. He emphasizes the Christian concept of "loving the sinner and hating the sin. "Correction", he states, "must be done out of love". https://www.devinemercy.org.

Christianity shaped European culture. Should Christian values be preserved as society moves into a future of social change under the European Union? Should Christianity be expected to decrease with a view of progress and change? Consider these issues as we move forward in the examination of history and the development of Europe and European culture.

Many countries have eliminated any reference to God, and Christianity, from their constitutions. Treaties of the European Union are no exception. Christians view this movement with alarm, and view with a sense of foreboding, consequences that could be in store for Europe. If God is not referred to for direction and support, God will not interfere or intervene in human affairs. When humanity is left to manage affairs independent of the God as Christians know him, catastrophe may result. Relativism, a belief that any behavior is acceptable, as long as it is right for the person forming the action, is used to base legal action. With respect to legislation and morality, without Christianity, rules become independent of good and evil. Through eliminating the word "God" in the European Union documents, the concept of human dignity is deprived of a real foundation. The protection of people and their rights, and respect for the human person, in practice, would not be considered. Politicians or lawyers hold the category of dignity hostage to its interpretation. Pseudo-laws, which destroy human dignity, are adopted in accordance with the law, and contrary to dignity. Because there is no reference to nature or to God, laws are formulated which consider a person as being a sovereign entity. This person, independent of a God, is left to choose happiness according impulse and not a moral standard. Good and evil are chosen, according to one's own whim. An extreme example may be terrorism, which could become acceptable if the act was done according to what is right for the person and not society.

Today, it is popular to renounce Christianity and Christian doctrine. The European Union advocates secularism. At one time, change came about through revolution. Democratic methods now seek to create change. The right to freedom guaranteed for all, only applies to those who accept the status quo.

The Ideology of the Enlightenment has led to the destruction of normal family life, and normal human development. In our current generation, many view the decline of the family as evidenced through high divorce rates, and the large number of children living in single parent homes.

Laws as they are formulated today threaten the most fundamental human rights, mainly for a Christian. People may no longer feel security in their own home country. People, instead, feel afraid, cornered and threatened. Christianity, at one time, represented the foundation of legal order. The most important right at one time was the right to life. This minimum, the right to life, can be denied. The legalization of abortion[218] and

---

218 We recognize that the issues involving abortion and euthanasia are multifaceted. Those involved on a personal level with these issues may experience great pain, both physical and emotional, and are never to be judged or condemned. It is beyond the scope of this book to explain or defend either position.
It is mentioned in a philosophical context regarding the rights in democracy of the people involved, the weak and vulnerable, versus the strong and powerful. One should not forget that the feelings of pain or joy are not the most fundamental criteria to decide what in reality is good or wrong for a human being as a person.
What is important between those who are either for or against abortion, is common ground. Both groups advocate for the woman's and the child's best interests. How to achieve this varies. A woman (and man) may have a sense of relief immediately following an abortion. The long-term effects can be devastating. As a trauma therapist for many years, the co-author (Lindael), has witnessed firsthand the emotional and psychological effects stemming from abortions. These effects are called Post Abortion Syndrome. The woman often suffers from low self-esteem, have nightmares, difficulty resting, be in constant activity, feel guilt, anxiety, depression, the list is ongoing …., yet not realize these symptoms are due to the abortion. Healing ministries have been developed by Christians to assist people to cope with the aftermath of some decisions that bring lifelong heartache. Rachel's vineyard is one such healing program developed through the Catholic Church. ; Rachel's Vineyard provides non-judgemental healing programs for those affected by abortion https://www.rachel'svineyard.org;
Pro Life Arguments for Secular Audiences. https:// www.frc.org.
Society does not permit cruelty to animals. It is recommended that the reader research abortion procedures. The "fetus" is subjected to painful procedures, again beyond the scope of this book, but strongly recommended for the readers further study. One example is the documentary "the Silent Scream". Another position to consider in the debate, is the moral issue concerning the child's natural right to live, the real being who came into existence, and who is lost. Next comes the debate at what point in fetus gestation is the fetus considered to be a baby. Pro-life advocates believe a baby is a child at the moment of conception. Pro-abortion advocates believe the "fetus" is not a baby until it has been born. Some Countries allow for the killing of the fetus just before birth. The

euthanasia[219], serve as examples of a law serving to deny the rights of a select group of the population, and serve as examples of a culture of death, not life. Other rights flow from this most fundamental right. Other rights, when the right to life is obliterated, mean nothing. Culture and civilization also mean nothing. Christianity at one time served as a foundation of creating legal order. The consequences of renouncing Christianity, may only lead to both devastation of a culture and of civilization.

Actions serving against the dignity of the human person could include co-habitation without marriage, homosexual unions, and the promotion of gender neutrality.[220] These issues are "hot topics" in our current culture. The catechism of the catholic faith explicitly defines responsibilities of Catholics to value, respect, and love all persons, regardless of life choices.[221] No one is to be judged or condemned because of actions contrary to Christian principles. Christians believe these choices, although they may seem to bring a happiness in ones current life situation, may not bring long

---

Voice of John, " www.voiceofjohn.org" is a powerful documentary worth the readers attention.

Again, beyond the scope of this book, but worth the readers further research, and reflection.

Another question for the reader's reflection: In the child's best interests, is the child better suited to being killed (aborted) or born? These go beyond the scope of this book.

219 A powerful video documentary titled "the Euthanasia deception" is well worth the readers further study. Belgium has had legalized euthanasia for many years now. It is horrifying to learn about the progression of a society bent upon killing anything that is no longer perfect. https://www.euthanasia.com; https://www.youtube.com.

220 The Catechism of the catholic church, number 2358 states the following: "The number of men and women who have deep-seated homosexual tendencies is not negligible. This inclination [............], constitutes for most of them a trial. They must be accepted with respect, compassion, and sensitivity. Every sign of unjust discrimination in their regard should be avoided. These persons are called to fulfill God's will in their lives and, if they are Christians, to unite to the sacrifice of the Lord's Cross the difficulties they may encounter from their condition". Brandon Vogt (claritasu.com: homosexuality) states: There is a distinction between a person's identity and actions; and between attraction (which is unintentional), and a person's behavior.

221 Love refers to a "choice", and not necessarily referring to a "feeling".

term happiness, may be the cause of many personal long term problems, and may not assist a person in their progress towards eternal life.

We emphasize here that we are mentioning these issues as philosophical concepts, and not political issues to debate or solve.

Christians who do not support current standards and laws that violate Christian principles are not treated with respect. Secularists target Christians. Christian beliefs are not respected or valued. These beliefs in some situations are openly condemned, and ridiculed. It becomes more advantageous to take actions against Christians than to respect the rights of Christians. The meaning of freedom only applies to those who accept secular beliefs and actions.[222]

The European Union and Freedom

The definition of freedom began to change. Being free, in this new concept of freedom, meant to take on secularism and reject Christianity. How did this come about?

Hostility is increasing toward Christians in the world as a whole. This attitude is not unique to the new Europe developing through the European Union. Pope Benedict XVI (2005–2013), when he was then known as Cardinal Joseph Ratzinger, described society as ruled by: "A dictatorship of relativism which does not recognize anything as definitive, and whose

---

222 The Ottawa Sun Newspaper: On October 31, 2018, an 85 year old priest was arrested in Ottawa Canada, because he stood outside an abortion clinic (within the 50 metre "bubble zone" protecting clinics under the " Safe Access to Abortion Services Act",) with a sign that made no reference to abortion, to the clinic, or pro-life, or contained graphic images that have bothered clients in the past.The sign simply said "The Primacy Of Free Speech/ Cornerstone of Western Civilization," while the other said "Without Free Speech/The State Is A Corpse." People being charged with a crime, or being put in jail, for quietly and respectfully expressing opinions contrary to the status quo, is becoming all too common. Many of these events are not publicized widely. If one has an interest and does research, much is to be found. For example, see CBNNews.com: "Canadian Christian faces jail time for expressing his beliefs at a Gay Pride Event". Further discussion of these events are beyond the scope of this book.

ultimate goal consists solely of satisfying the desires of one's own ego."[223] Pope Benedict also said: "one of the central problems of the 21st Century, is relativism, which is a denial of objective truth".[224] In another address, (Berlin 2000), Pope Benedict noted the disparity in the tolerance towards religion. The opinions of Christians are not tolerated, as contrasted towards the religious tolerance towards Judaism and Islam:

> "My final point has to do with the religious issue. I wouldn't want to get involved in the complex debates so recurrent over the past few years, but rather highlight just one aspect fundamental for all cultures: respect for what is sacred for someone else: most especially, respect for sacredness in the loftiest sense, respect for God. If this respect fails to be observed, whoever dishonours the faith of Israel, its image of God and its great personages, is liable to punishment in the form of a fine. The same applies to anyone who publicly insults the Koran and the fundamental tenets of Islam. When it is a matter of Christ and what is sacred for Christians, however, freedom of opinion emerges as the supreme good and any limitation thereof is said to threaten or even destroy tolerance and freedom in general. And yet this is exactly where we see the limit of freedom of speech: it may not destroy the honor and dignity of anyone else. Freedom of speech is not the freedom to voice falsehoods or destroy human rights."[225]

And as a cardinal Joseph Ratzinger earlier explained:

> "Nowadays, practically no one would directly contest the precedence of human dignity and fundamental human rights with respect to any political decision; all too recent are the horrors of Nazism and its racial policy. In the concrete area of the so-called progress of medicine, however, there subsist very real threats for these values: when we think of things such as cloning, or the conservation of human fetuses for purposes of research and organ donation, or the vast field of genetic manipulation, the slow consumption threatening human dignity cannot be disregarded by anyone at all. Added to this, in ever-increasing magnitude, is the trafficking of human beings, the new forms of slavery, the trafficking of human organs for transplants. Ever trumpeted are good ends in an effort to justify what can in no way be justified."[226]

---

223 Homily of his Eminence Card. Joseph Ratzinger Dean of the College of Cardinals, Vatican, 18 April, 2005: 8 May 2018 http://www.vatican.va/gpII/documents/homily-pro-eligendo-pontifice_20050418_en.html.
224 Ratzinger, *Homily*.
225 Ratzinger, *Europe: Its Spiritual Foundation: Yesterday, Today and in the Future*. May 13 2004. Adress to the Italian Senate: 8 May 2018.
226 Ratzinger, *Europe*.

And then cardinal Ratzinger explained possible reasons for the growth and acceptance of Islam:

> "The rebirth of Islam is connected not only with the new material wealth of the Islamic countries, but is nourished by Islam's ability to offer sound spiritual grounds for the life of peoples, grounds which seem to have slipped out of Europe's steady hand. Therefore, despite its lasting political and economic might, Europe is increasingly looked upon as condemned to its decline and downfall."[227]

As we continue to describe Europe, we refer to the West and the East. Poland is in the middle of Europe. All countries to the north, south or west of Poland are called western countries, including the largest countries of Italy, France, Germany, Spain, Austria, and Switzerland. These countries are classified as West because of their culture, history and civilization, and not because of their geography.

Russia is in the Eastern part of Europe and is in Asia. In the decades prior to 1989–1990, Eastern European countries were called countries belonging to the Soviet Union. Currently the situation has changed and Russia is the country referred to when one is referring to Eastern Europe.

Europe, in its recent past, has experienced much upheaval. Cardinal Ratzinger discussed a possible symptom connected with its stormy past. The West is experiencing a current lack of European self-esteem:

> Here in the West there are strange forms of self-hate we can only consider pathological. Yes, in a rather praiseworthy manner, the West does strive to be open in full to the comprehension of external values, but it no longer loves itself. All it sees in its own history is what is disgraceful and destructive, while it no longer seems able to perceive what is great and pure. In order to survive, Europe needs a new, critical and humble acceptance of itself; but only if it really wishes to survive. The multi-culturalism now being encouraged and fostered with such passion comes across at times as mostly an abandonment and denial of what is one's own, a sort of flight from self.[228]

Cardinal Ratzinger attributed this low self-esteem to a European memory. Europe had a history of destruction and disgrace from its past. Europe no longer seems able to perceive what is great and pure. This is the way a European person experiences living in Europe. Non-Europeans may

---

227 Ratzinger, *Europe.*
228 Ratzinger, *Europe.*

not perceive this; this is something that can only be perceived as personal experience.

In discussing this self-hate further, European self-hate started and continued under the impact of the following theologies: anti-rationalism, anti-realism, volunteerism, anti-Catholicism through Protestantism, and then anti Christianity through Atheism. Anti-rationalism was a theory that was promoted during the Middle Ages by the Gnostic sects, (Cathars, Albigenses, etc.).[229] Anti-realism started in the period of late medieval nominalism. The essence of being a real being was declared to be an empty concept. Voluntarism refers to a will that has priority, the will over emotion or reason.

These controversies were discussed not only with a very strong emotional fervor; they also had immense consequences for social life, including theology. Finally, the new concept of Europe, based upon protestant assumptions, started to be built in opposition to the Greek, Roman and Catholic heritage of the past. Opposition was expressed with a strong emotional disregard, which can be called hate. As time progressed, the protestant religion was substituted by an ideology of liberal atheism. New modern Europe looked to hate the old Europe. For Europeans, this continues into the present.

For Cardinal Ratzinger, Europe's self-hate may be explained by the following: In contemporary Europe, many aspects of European identity, which have been developing for centuries, the ones that are labeled as being Greek, Roman and Christian, are not only neglected, deemed invalid, and rejected, but they are also simply hated. These include Objective Truth, Objective Good, Objective Beauty, and the Real Christ as being humanity's Savior. A contemporary identity of the Europe of the present is based upon relativism and nihilism. This has a disastrous effect. The effect is to make Europe alien to itself.

Europe's self-hate becomes pathological (a mental disorder), because it is not normal to not like oneself. What is normal is to love one's own

---

229 The Cathars (Albigenses) were a heretical Christian sect in western Europe in the 12th and 13th centuries. They believed in the dualism of two principles, one good and the other evil, the material world being evil. https://www.britannica.com

identify and those of others, based upon the Christian principle of love your neighbor as you love yourself.[230]

Cardinal Ratzinger in this same address discussed secularism in the modern world:

> "History was no longer to be gauged on the basis of an idea of God which preceded it and gave it form. Statehood was looked upon in purely secular terms, based on rationality and the will of citizens. Witnessed for absolutely the first time in history was the emergence of a completely secular or non-denominational state, which abandoned and set aside the divine warranty and divine regulation of the political element, considering such elements as belonging to a mythical vision of the world. In addition, such a state declared God Himself to be a private matter, belonging to neither the sphere of public life nor the common formation of civic volition. The latter was considered to be solely a matter of reason, with respect to which God did not appear clearly knowable."[231]

In other words, religion and faith in God were postulated to belong in the sphere of feelings, and not that of reason. God and His will ceased to have any relevance in public life.

The Enlightenment brought about a secularization of Europe. By the turn of the twentieth and twenty-first centuries, an anti-Christian attitude became dominant in contemporary Europe. A program aimed at the de-Christianization of Europe advanced and grew, while the other two monotheistic religions, Judaism and Islam, were not criticized. Moreover, the anti-Christian attitude was deemed a necessary and major expression of being a European.

---

230 "and you shall love the Lord your God with all your heart, and with all your soul, and with all your mind, and with all your strength.' The second is this, 'You shall love your neighbor as yourself.' There is no other commandment greater than these". This scripture gives instructions about loving God and others Mark 12: 30–31 *the New Revised Standard Version Bible, Catholic Edition (NRSVCE)*, copyright © 1989, 1993 the Division of Christian Education of the National Council of the Churches of Christ in the United States of America. Used by permission. All rights reserved: https://www.biblegateway.com/theNewRevisedStandardVersionBible/CatholicEdition (RESVCE).

231 Ratzinger, *Europe.*

An anti – Christian attitude was equated with the concept of being free. Being free was equated with being European. Being free required the adoption of an anti-Christian attitude. Being free was an attitude promoted as a strategy to destroy Christianity.

Being anti-Christian became fashionable. This fashion was shaped through the worship of celebrities (actors, singers, and some politicians) who actively supported anti-Christianity in their public life.

Although Christians are often ostracized because of their opposition to behaviors that were becoming mainstream in society, this was not the main cause of their rejection.

Christians attempted to protect ethics, moral codes, and principles. Christians were in opposition to mainstream secularism, which they believed would cause negative consequences in public and professional life. Christians needed to be silenced. This silencing of Christians became possible due to the attitude of political correctness. Political correctness allowed for a personal freedom of conscience, where the state and the church (a love for God) were not to be joined. The age of relativism began. Any behaviour or whim inspired an individual is permissible. The age of relativism emerged. Christians were against Relativism, which carries an anti-Christian attitude. Relativism holds that truth is subjective; moral or religious principles have no value, or, if they do have value, they have value for the individual, and not for a people as a whole. Ethical truths are dependent upon individual perceptions or viewpoints. The best interests of the culture or peoples living within it merit less value than individual whims, wants or desires. Examples of relativistic language include: It is right (or not right) for me. Relativistic thinking is common in our culture. Christians support the notion of an objective truth, believing relativistic thinking to be dangerous. My "truth", my view, the view which I hold as being true, could in reality be quite detrimental for the individual, the family, or the culture in which I belong.

Christianity was a religion that for centuries had saved Europe. Christianity had shaped Europe's cultural identity. Christianity was the basis of the European culture. The new concept of freedom turned against Europe's historical past.

Pope John Paul II (1978 to 2005) made repeated appeals, requesting a clear statement about the Christian roots of the European continent to be included in the Treaty that established a Constitution for Europe. His request was not satisfied.[232]

The direction and shaping of the European Union became more and more anti-Christian, both in the religious and moral sphere. Beginning with the Maastricht Treaty, documents were signed in the process of European integration. These documents did not directly appose Christianity. However, Christianity was not mentioned. Avoiding any mention of Europe's Christian roots and influence in treaty documents would be an effective initial strategy to de Christianize Europe.

The Amsterdam treaty was the next treaty to escalate the anti-Christian movement in Europe. The Amsterdam treaty creates confusion, and this is perhaps, not accidental. In trying to decipher this treaty, one becomes lost in reading the text. A final version is difficult to find. Improvements upon improvements upon improvements obscure any final understanding of its contents.

The Amsterdam treaty specifically contravenes Christian Scripture. For Christians, the language and specific clauses located within the treaty signaled a beginning of Europe's De-Christianization. Article 2 of the Amsterdam Treaty refers to the strategy of gender mainstreaming.[233] This clause opens the way to a full de-Christianization of Europe in moral and religious spheres. This opened the way to De-Christianization for Christians because it contravenes scripture. Christians refer to their Bible, when planning future direction. Christians also believe that, by contravening scripture and the social teaching of the church, the laws that God gave humanity, all will collapse. In specifically referring to the Christian bible: God created a person to be either a man or a woman, God decided upon a person's

---

232 *Address of His Holiness Pope John Paul II to the Former Stagiaires of the Robert Schuman Foundation*, 7.11.2003: 8 May 2018 https://w2.vatican.va/content/john-paul-ii/en/speeches/2003/november/documents/hf_jp-ii_spe_20031107_robert-schuman.html.

233 The article on the website explains how the gender mainstreaming strategy works: *Mainstreaming Gender in the European Union – Jean Monnet Center*: 11 May 2018 www.jeanmonnetprogram.org/archive/papers/00/000201.rtf.

gender before that person was born.[234] God did not create humans as neutral objects who would later decide to be either man or woman. Upon this conviction is built family and society.

Gender Mainstreaming and the European Union

Much literature in this secular world supports gender neutrality. Christians threaten the ideology of the current culture. The Convention of the Council of Europe (May 2001) followed the Amsterdam Treaty. This council met with the intention of formulating a plan for the protection of women from violence, and to enact laws to provide for gender equality. The purpose of gender equality is to allow for equal opportunity and wage parody for all people, regardless of whether a person is born male or female.

In reality, the focus of the convention was Gender mainstreaming. Gender neutrality is an ideology rooted in Marxism and Neo-Marxism. Although equality is a positive goal, mainstreaming is not positive, when considered in the perspective of Christian theology and ethics. Equality allows equal rights to all people. Mainstreaming is an attempt to make all people the same.

Relativism is the current worldview, believing in a subjective versus an objective truth. For the relativist, any behavior becomes permissible, if it is in line with a person's own view of truth. Taken to the extreme, murder and terrorism become acceptable.

In the Christian perspective, there is an objective truth. Murder, as an objective truth, is morally wrong. Christians base their understanding about what is right and what is wrong upon Scripture. This scripture gives instruction according to what a divine and all loving God has told his people, and what can be confirmed by rationally knowing reality. God designed men and women to be different from each other, each having unique gifts and

---

234 "So God created humankind in his image, in the image of God he created them; male and female he created them". Genesis 1: 27 *the New Revised Standard Version Bible, Catholic Edition (NRSVCE)*, copyright © 1989, 1993 the Division of Christian Education of the National Council of the Churches of Christ in the United States of America. Used by permission. All rights reserved: https://www.biblegateway.com/theNewRevisedStandardVersionBible/CatholicEdition (RESVCE).

strengths that the other does not possess. The difference in gender between man and woman for the Christian is essential, not accidental, not artificial, nor are these differences conventional. Gender is objective, not subjective. The unique difference and strengths between a man and a woman are given by nature, and from God himself. What was at one time a goal striving towards equality and fairness, allows now for the confusion and uncertainty about one's own self and nature. Confusion is not of God.

Gender mainstreaming is not the same as equality. Equality is not the same as identity. When people have the option to make decisions about their gender, deciding about which gender one is to become, gender itself is in danger of becoming distorted because it has taken on a subjective and not objective reality. The consequences may be fatal. Christian western culture and religion become a human decision. When the gender identity of a person is imposed, then they are aspiring to be something that is not true. Simplifying this concept, if a person thinks their hand does not belong to them; therapy aims to correct this person's distorted body image, not to remove the hand surgically. If a person believes they are an animal, they are not surgically changed to be an animal. If a person believes themselves to be a quadriplegic, the spinal cord is not severed to create an "accurate" body image. However, if a person believes their gender is not correct, surgery aims to make a correction, rather than assisting the person through therapy to develop the correct body image.[235]

Promotion and legalization of gender neutrality through the European Union conventions, indicates how far the European Union strayed from its Christian heritage and principles. The basis of the European Union was to protect the dignity of the human as a person. Human dignity is no longer protected. The Roman Catholic Church explicitly criticized the documents of the convention because of their apparent anti-Christian character in political, religious, and moral spheres. The European Union ignores the

---

235 Brandon Vogt, discusses hot issues and puts them in a context understandable and clear. In his series regarding transgenderism, he discusses the intent of "surgical correction" to prevent suicides. After a 20-year longitudinal study, the suicide rate had not decreased in spite of these surgeries. https://claritasu. com/courses.

history of a civilization that developed in order to preserve human dignity. The founding Fathers of the European Union warned against this.

Christians view the current evolving worldview, and legislation of Gender ideology, as a direct attack on gender, the family, western culture, religion, civilization as we know it, and upon Christianity. Gender neutrality undermines the biological nature of human sexuality; it rejects marriage as being a voluntary and sacramental relationship between two people of different sexes; and it violates the nature and function of a normal family, which is open to having and raising their children. At one time the family functioned to fulfil a specific role in both the biological and social spheres.

De-Christianization affects society, and the individual within it. When a person accepts the current worldview as proposed by the European Union, that person is deprived of a reference to the transcendental and supernatural. It denies a person of that which constitutes his or her personhood in terms of one's nature and rights. The ideology of the European Union deliberately seeks the destruction of Europe in both biological and cultural spheres.[236] Bringing Europe under the control of the ideology of globalization may aim to depart from existing national states. The outcome may be to denationalize societies and for the sovereignty of historical states to be lost.

It took thousands of years for European identity to be developed. What it means to be European is being eroded through the concept of a Europe that is being developed within the European Union. Traditional Europeanness had two central foundations: family and faith. Organizational and legal structures are being put into place devised to weaken, and then destroy these two central foundations. The battle for Europe continues, only now it is fought against faith, the family, and about what is right and wrong.

Federation or Federative Europe

In striving towards creating a united Europe, a variety of factors need to be considered, developed and implemented. How have these been implemented and what does this mean for the Europe of the past?

---

236 Marguerite A. Peeters, *Le gender: une norme politique et culturelle mondiale. Outil de discernement* (Paris: Mame, 2012).

There were justifiable reasons to unify Europe, especially the desire for peace. Europe had experienced too many wars. However, in order to politically unify Europe, Europe needed to agree upon the format of this unification. Europe could either become united into one country, or, Europe could form an association of countries.

If Europe were to become one Federal country, the sovereignty and autonomy of Member states would be renounced. Europe would become a Superstate. National sovereignty would be relinquished in favor of one central office, which would include all the Member States.[237] The problem of national egoism and antagonism would be solved if this were the direction Europe would choose to go.[238] However, it would need to be carried out delicately, step by step.[239] The Founding Fathers (Schuman, de Gasperi, Adenauer) leaned towards this model of a united Europe, in spite of their hesitations about possible negative future outcomes.

If Europe were to form an association of Countries and become a Federative Europe, the sovereignty of the individual countries would be preserved. Europe would become a Europe of Homelands. Limits upon the integration of states would be established. The sovereignty of states of historical origin would be preserved. Charles de Gaulle (1890–1970) was a general during World War Two, and later became a president of France. His political ideology has become a major influence in French politics. He was a great supporter of Europe becoming an association of countries.

In recent years, the creation of one Federal European Superstate has been the dominant trend in the political arena. However, there are a number of obstacles, which would need to be overcome. Problems to be resolved include: 1: Developing and obtaining support for the adoption of a European constitution from those wanting to preserve their unique heritage of the past; 2: Managing and reconciling the effects of the developing trend towards Liberalism 3: Culture, Language and History: Finding creative solutions in preserving nationality as a historical and cultural category; 4: Traditions, history, culture: deciding which would be preserved, lost, or replaced with modern and different ones; 5: Making decisions about what

---

237 Wahl, *Robert Schumann*, p. 50.
238 Wahl, *Robert Schumann*, p. 52.
239 Wahl, *Robert Schumann*, p. 38.

the relationship would entail between the state or nation with the super state; 6: Deciding how much autonomy versus the loss of autonomy, that each of the various states would have. Finding methods to determine how much autonomy that each nation would have, and developing methods to make these decisions; 7: Determining which politics and which ideologies were to be implemented from the wide range of philosophical systems available. These included: liberalism versus religion, right versus left wing actions, socialism, personalism, secularization, democracy, totalitarianism, religious systems and practices of the past, including Christianity, the list continues. Europe has come from a rich history of varying and conflicting political agendas and philosophical belief systems. A great challenge was before the involved nations and political leaders, in reconciling these challenges with each other.

Formulating a Constitution

If Europe were to form one Federal European Superstate, officials would be required to obtain sufficient support from the people. Next, a constitution would need to be developed. In the 1950's, Europe wasn't supportive of forming itself into a Superstate too hastily. Instead of using the emotionally charged word constitution in speeches and documents, other words were used instead. The words Political Statute, and then Constitutional Act, were the words used in the Treaty Establishing a Constitution for Europe (2004). The concept of a European Union continues to be complex. Political party agendas, and social concepts, remain unclear, as these treaties are being developed and implemented.

Sufficient support to accepting the one Federal European Superstate proved to be a difficult challenge. Not all Member States had decided to ratify the Treaty. Of the twenty-seven Member States, seventeen parliaments voted to accept the treaty. This treaty had been initially accepted by 63 % of the member states. However, when we consider the national referendums, only four referendums were organized, two States voted to accept the treaty (Spain, 20/02/2005, Luxembourg, 10/07/2005), and two States voted against it: France (29/00/2005) and the Netherlands (0/06/2005). Without sufficient support for the treaty, the ratification process for a European Constitution halted.

The Agenda and Philosophy of Liberalism

Political leaders and philosophers did not give up in their quest to form a Superstate.

Historically, the German philosopher, Immanuel Kant, supported the idea of a single super state.

Kant wrote an essay about a program designed to bring about perpetual peace entitled *"Zumewigen Frieden"* (1795).[240]

The continued problem in creating a Superstate remained with the issue of sovereignty and how to obtain public support. Sovereignty would be renounced by any nation and state that would be in favor of renouncing their individual entity in favor of the single super state.

The idea of a super state is rooted in liberalism, a political philosophy founded on equality, freedom, gender equality, and international cooperation. Liberalism when examined in relation to both the individual, and the state, is based on a false premise. Liberalism distorts the understanding of the structure and function of both humans and society. A person, by their very nature, is always free, responsible for their own decisions. People always have a right to happiness. The government may be democratically elected, or formed into a dictatorship, yet, freedom is not surrendered to the government.

The issue of justice may be considered. Justice is the legal or philosophical virtue by which fairness is administered. Three of these types of justice may be examined through the works of Thomas Aquinas, and include: distributive justice, contributive (general) justice, and commutative justice.[241] Josef Pieper (1904 – 1997) defines these three forms of justice succinctly. "When may justice be said to prevail in a nation?" asks Pieper. Following St. Thomas, Pieper answers that, "justice rules in a community or state whenever the three basic relations, the three fundamental structures of communal life, are disposed in their proper order": the relations of

---

240 *The History of the Idea of Europe*, p. 76–77. This view was supported by, among others, writer Victor Hugo, who claimed that Paris should be the capital of the new European country. Ibid.

241 "Thomas Aquinas – Moral Philosophy", in: *Internet Encyclopedia of Philosophy*: 8 May 2018 http://www.iep.utm.edu/aq-moral/.

individuals to one another (commutative justice); the relations of the social whole to individuals (distributive justice); and the relations of individuals to the social whole (legal or general justice)."[242] Regardless of the differing viewpoints and relationships between contributive (legal), commutative, and distributive justice, justice is about fairness in giving a person that which is deserved. A person is the aim when considering rules about fairness, not society. Society is a set of relations between people who have the status of a substance. Society is only a relationship in a metaphysical sense. For this reason, and, in the end, society exists for a person, a person does not exist for society.

Culture, Language and History

Those involved in European Union treaties, aimed to prevent any upheaval that could turn into protests against a united Europe. Protests were to be avoided by implementing a slow, step-by-step integration strategy. This strategy implemented a new administrative category into European Union documents. European countries were given the administrative category of European regions. The concept of homeland was replaced by the categories of national sovereignty and state independence. Common culture, language and history were set aside or were treated instrumentally.[243] An artificial unity was created in order to make modifications to the agreement, in order to prevent major objections. The aim was to lead toward a merger of the nations into the structure of the European Union. The Europe of regions

---

242 https://www.thecatholicthing.org/2018/06/06/the-three-forms-of-justice/.

243 Today, the category of region could mean one of three things: 1. The category of a region could represent a unit that is smaller than the country, including the current or historical province. An example would be a Podlasie. A Podlasie, or Podlachia, is an historical region in the eastern part of Poland. 2. The category of a region could be represented as a unit that is established based upon the cooperation of several countries. For example, the Visegrad Group, which includes the Czech Republic, Slovakia, Hungary and Poland; 3. The category of a region could be represented as networks of cooperating border units such as would be portrayed as provinces or cities. Euroregion Bug is an example of this type of region. It includes the Lubelskie Voivodeship in Poland, Volyn Oblast, two regions in the Lviv Oblast in Ukraine and Brest Oblast in Belarus. Boer, *The History of the Idea of Europe*, p. 195.

was implemented in order to create a transitional phase that would lead towards the Federation of Europe, the Superstate.

Traditions, History and Culture

The next agenda of the organizing committee of the Union was to distance and disintegrate both individuals and society from their traditional, historical, and cultural relationships. For this to occur, the state and the homeland would need to become secondary to the European Union. The category of "little homeland," was introduced to give a new meaning to the word homeland. Little homeland would now be used to refer to cities, towns, or districts. Little homeland would become a dependent entity, and it was hoped that its identity could in time, be changed or lost.

There are two conditions that could lead to the cultural identity of a little homeland being lost. The first condition includes the creation of partitions, colonialism or neo-colonialism. Colonialism refers to a method of gaining control over a country through occupying it with settlers, and by acquiring its goods unfairly. Neocolonialism refers to the dominance of a stronger nation over a weaker one by economic and cultural means. These methods may be used when a foreign country rules over another country, and used when these differing countries do not have a shared history.

The second condition that would allow for the loss of cultural identity would be for a larger state to control, restrain, and to create a dependency of this smaller entity upon it.

Changing the significance of the term little homeland continued to be a strategy implemented. The term little homeland could carry an emotional tie, but it would now only be important if it were referred to in relation to a large homeland, which is the large state. Little homeland now would become a dependent entity. Its identity could then be changed and, or, lost, which could happen if it were organized into the European Union.

New politics of memory and new ideological priorities were next introduced. Rather than promoting historical falsehoods (as in totalitarian systems), the rich European history would be concealed. New concepts of man, woman, family, and society, were introduced. These concepts were inconsistent with biology, culture and religion, but went unnoticed. A framework setting regulatory and administrative limits was used, that was based upon one utopian project.

Postmodernism supports this process.[244] Postmodernism is a philosophy that was introduced in the late twentieth century. Social progress, absolute truth and objective reality, were all discarded. Knowledge and truth are instead now believed to be products of social, historical and political interpretations. These interpretations now become contextual, the meaning of the event relating to the circumstance, and socially construed.

Inter Relationships: State, Nation, Superstate

The public had cause to be concerned about the draft of the European Constitution. This draft would allow for the potential loss of both political sovereignties, and of national identity.[245]

As with liberalism, the relationship between the states with the super state (the nation with the super nation) is based upon a false premise. The European Union as a Superstate is created mainly by an administrative decision, and threatens the culture and historical sovereignty of nationality.

Nationality, expressed through the mother tongue, determines the context of an individual's life. In this context, generations work towards a national society. An individual expresses oneself to the fullest, when he belongs to a society and nation with a rich memory of history and culture.[246]

---

244 Boer, *The History of the Idea of Europe*, p. 207.

245 Sociological studies of Spanish society show that most Spaniards are in favor of the European integration, but not at the expense of losing national identity. 37 % of respondents think about themselves as Spaniards only, 59 % as Spaniards and Europeans, and only 4 % as Europeans only. Therefore, the vast majority (96 %) does not want to give up their national identity, and more than a half of respondents (59 %) claim that being European does not require giving up national identity. Jaquín Jareño Alarcón, "Identidad y ciudadanía en la nueva Europa. Algunos motivos para reflexión," in: *Miradas sobre Europa*, eds. Joaquín Jareño Alarcón, Miguel Ángel García Olmo (Murcia: Fundación Universitaria San Antonio, 2006), p. 192.

246 The deepest understanding of the category of the nation cannot be underestimated, the category that reaches the level of a person's discovery of one's own humanity. This is done in the context of a national life community, and not just in the economic or political community. St. Pope John Paul II

Autonomy versus Autonomy Loss

One now begins to wonder whether it is possible for the countries of Europe to create a structure of states, a Superstate, modeled upon the structure of the United States. Advantages of this model are examined as a possible structure for Europe to consider. The flaws that still remain in the current proposal are examined.

The current structure of the United States, used as a model for the developing European Union, would not be an effective model to implement. Europe is made up of countries rich in their own history, language, tradition, political systems, and geography. Each country continues to desire autonomy in order to preserve a rich cultural history that is centuries old.[247] It would be impossible for individual European nations to stop

---

repeatedly drew special attention to this. Krystyna Czuba, *Idea Europy kultur w nauczaniu Jana Pawła II* [*Concept of Europe of cultures in the teachings of John Paul II*], (Warsaw: Wydawnictwo Soli Deo, 2003), pp. 90–1. The speech he delivered at the United Nations on 4th October 1995 in New York was especially important – John Paul 11 called for the U.N. to strongly consider the demand for preparing such an international agreement. The international agreement, which is modeled on the Universal Declaration of Human Rights, (1948) would cover the rights of nations. The first is the nations' individual right to exist, and following the nations right to exist, is a nations' right to maintain their native language and culture, to build their future, and to educate their youth. Address of His Holiness John Paul II, United Nations Headquarters, New York Thursday 5 October 1995: 8 May 2017 https://w2.vatican.va/content/john-paul-ii/en/speeches/1995/october/documents/hf_jp-ii_spe_05101995_address-to-uno.html The question arises – does the European Union take into consideration the welfare and rights of nations in their anthropological and cultural aspect, and not only in ethnic or political aspect?

247 Charles de Gaulle pointed out this fundamental difference between the United States and Europe: "In this respect what is true of economics is even truer of politics. And this is no more than natural. What depths of illusion or prejudice would have to be plumbed in order to believe that European nations forged through long centuries by endless exertion and suffering, each with its own geography, history, language, traditions and institutions, could cease to be themselves and form a single entity? What a perfunctory view is reflected in the parallel often naïvely drawn between what Europe ought to do and what the United States have done, when the latter was created from nothing in a completely new territory by successive waves of uprooted colonists." Charles

being themselves. A model based on the United States would be impractical and shallow. Such a draft proposal has been developed for the European Union. This draft is yet to be approved. There are numerous other reasons why a model based upon that of the United States would be ill advised for the E.U. to follow. There are numerous differences between the current Europe, and what constituted the communities of the United States in 1776, when it formally became the United States of America. In 1776 the United states became a new nation as formulated in the U.S. declaration of Independence. Communities of the United States were of migrant origin. Yet, when the original constitution of the United States was ratified, individual state autonomy was included in their constitution. Each state has its own constitution and a number of powers independent from the central government. From the historical perspective, it must be noted that the United States Constitution would not have been approved by the individual states if the Constitution had not guaranteed that the federal government would not take complete control over the states.

Ten amendments to the Bill of Rights were added because of fear of, and to prevent Federal Government domination. The ninth and tenth amendments, ratified in 1791, strongly emphasize that the rights of the individual state takes precedence over the rights of the federal government. This precedence had been respected for 120 years. Beginning during the presidency of Woodrow Wilson, the situation began to change whereby precedence is provided in favor of the federal government.[248] The struggle for greater autonomy of individual states in relation to their central government continues. The Supreme Court is involved in this struggle.

---

de Gaulle, *Memoirs of Hope. Renewal and Endeavor* (New York: Simon and Schuster, 1971), p. 189. That is why the phrase *United States of Europe* does not really suit Europe. It appeared in Victor Hugo's speeches in 1849 at the International Peace Congress in Paris and later in 1871 at the French National Assembly. See A. Sierra Gonzáles, "El constitucionalismo fallido de la Unión Europea," in: *Europa a examen. Nuevo diálogos sobre el Viejo Mundo*, ed. Alfonso, García Marqués, José Antonio García-Lorente (Madrid: Editorial Dykinson, 2013), p. 167.

248 28th president of the United States. He was in office between 1913 and 1921. https:/www.britannica.com.

Examining constitutions and bill of rights usage and development is critical, because one must assume the constitution is the basis of modern statehood. There are a number of important differences between the United States constitution and its bill of rights, compared with the proposed constitution for the European Union. These differences are difficult to reconcile. Differences include firstly the liberal versus socialist objectives; secondly the number of words and articles used (clarity of interpretation); and thirdly emphasis about the rights of its citizens.

Firstly, the draft constitution for the European Union went in an opposite direction to the formalized constitution and bill of rights developed and utilized in the United States. The United States document is liberal and right wing. The proposed document of the E.U. is an extremely socialist and left-wing document.

Secondly, the constitution of the United States is concise: The preamble is made up of 52 words, and the main text consists of 7 articles. At the time of writing, the preamble of the proposed E.U. Constitution contains 293 words and the main text contains more than 400 articles.

Thirdly, when examining the rights of citizens, the U.S. Constitution and Bill of Rights protects individual rights and justice, and places restrictions on the powers of the government. This U.S. document lists the obligations of the citizen towards the state. People in such a humanistic society decide to be together in order to have better and safe life, a life in which is impossible to accomplish through being alone or through living in a small group. Within this model, individuals have many obligations. The individual is required to build the society/state into a safe and better place to life. Because people within this model offer what they are able to the state, the state-society has reciprocal obligations towards its members, especially when the individuals are in poor condition and cannot do for themselves, alone, what they want or what they need. When obligations of the citizen towards the state are emphasized, there must be a special effort, organization, and agreement between individuals towards the state. The state in and by itself is not constituted and maintained by itself.

The European draft, rather than listing the obligations of the citizen towards the state, as the U.S. constitution does, it lists the obligations of the State towards the citizen. When obligations of the state towards the citizen are emphasized, the person, the citizen, and the citizen's rights, are given the priority. In the socialistic E.U. document that has been drafted, the individual is to work towards the state at some level. Socialism exists for the state. The individual has less value than the state does. The danger exists when the value of the individual decreases and becomes "lower and lower". In both models, that of the U.S. and the proposed E.U document, the citizen must work toward the state on some level. The difference between the two is based on the level or amount the person must work for the state. The individual in the socialist society at the extreme, exists for the state. In a liberal society, the level of individual requirement towards the state, on the continuum, is less. When a society moves towards the far left, the tendency of movement is towards more socialism, currently occurring with the E.U., whereby the state gives more and more to its citizens. The analogy, is "to give a person a fish, rather than a fishing rod". When the citizens become less able to manage their own life and affairs by themselves, the state goes into bankruptcy, as did the Soviet Union. When the state has a tendency towards allowing the individual to be more individually effective and self-managing, the state is in effect, as an analogy, giving the person a "rod" and not a "fish". The middle of the road stance, is to facilitate the person who can be self-sufficient, (the business executive) and to assist the one who is unable (the weak, ill, infirm). The catholic solution and perspective regarding the requirement of the individual in an obligation towards the state, is a mixture of both the right-wing and left-wing perspectives, or, one might say, in the middle of the continuum between right and left. The state and the individual exist in a reciprocal relationship. They each help and facilitate each other as they are able. The state and the individual do not leave each other alone, nor does one substitute or relinquish a power for each other.

The current proposal for the European Union contains many flaws. Problems include: citizenship; the method of introduction of the European state; marginalization; implemented ideologies conflicting with those of the people they are meant to serve; the role of migrants and immigrants; and; the foundation of culture and history that remain in conflict with current practices.

Citizenship is now based upon belonging to the new European nation. A history of identity is being lost. The European nation was introduced in a top–down manner, through educational, cultural, and media policy, and not through collaboration of the peoples of the nations. Economic policy aimed to speed up the process of a mixing of cultures and nations. People coming from nations rich in history are becoming marginalized due to this new civil society. Ideologies conflict: the ideologies that are being supported in this Union may not support the ideologies of the peoples to which it is meant to serve. Europe has seen an inflow of the immigrant labor force, not only from different countries, but also from different continents. This creates a movement in the labor market affecting the pan–European scale, and, migration policy. The role of these migrants and immigrants in this new society is not clearly defined, yet these newcomers may affect policy of the Union in ways that will seem offensive to those who do not share the foundation of the history, culture, and religion of the past, what and how it was developed. The Christian religion and Western culture constitute the main axis on which the European identity has been built.[249] New ideologies, that are forced upon the peoples, including the above-mentioned gender ideology, cause friction in an already strained union of states.

---

249 John Paul II referred to the need for the primacy of culture and religion over economy and geography: "In these times when the continent of Europe is undergoing profound transformations, *the witness of Christians takes on a renewed urgency*. It is important that the nations of this continent be helped to rediscover the deepest source of their culture, and of that civilization which makes it possible to speak of a European identity and to aspire to a unity which goes beyond merely geographical and economic considerations. That source is the Christian faith in which the peoples of Europe were baptized and confirmed, and from which they drew inspiration for their achievements and for their consciousness of the inalienable dignity of individuals as the basis of justice and peace in society. Perhaps as few times in the past, Europe needs to hear the reconciling word of the Gospel of our Lord Jesus Christ. All Christians must be committed to giving this witness, and as a fundamental part of it they must feel the urgency of following together those paths which will lead to overcoming our divisions. May God give us the strength to continue in this direction." *Address of His Holiness John Paul II at the Meeting of the Presbytery of Europe of the Church of Scotland*, 7 March 1992: https://w2.vatican.va/content/john-paul-ii/en/speeches/1992/march/documents/hf_jp-ii_spe_19920307_presbiterio-scozia.html.

Implementing Politics and Ideologies

Statements made about unity by the Founding Fathers of the European Union, were not entirely clear. One aim of a united Europe was to strengthen the security and prosperity of Europe through regulation and administration, processes that political systems provide. Another aim was to create a unification of the military. An opposite aim of a united Europe was to maintain Europe's high cultural heritage, to preserve a rich cultural history that was inherently imbedded in each of the national states. The founding fathers were unsettled in the cultural aspect. A formation of a European Union could have implications regarding the preservation of the unique cultures of the various countries involved.

The European culture has developed over time, in the nations. It was not formed in the abstract. The unique European culture could not exist without clinging to its rich historical roots. The founding Fathers were politicians of a high caliber. They were cognizant of the importance that religion played in terms of the European culture. They were aware that religion plays a role in the ultimate aim of life for individuals in society. The founding fathers wanted to resolve a key problem, the threat that the unique European culture could be lost. The founding fathers wanted to manage the security and prosperity of Europe, as well as to preserve the culture, history, and the role of religion in Europe. They recognized that managing these aspects incorrectly could lead to the future devastation of Europe.

Managing the integration of Europe was not an activity to be carried out by contemporary technocrats without a good humanistic education.[250] It cannot be carried out by those belonging to left-wing circles.[251] The

---

250 De Gaulle warned that a pan-European technocratic system would provide a huge advantage to Germany at the expense of other countries, especially France. For that reason, the General supported Europe to be a confederation of sovereign countries. W. Bokajło, *Koncepcja Europy*, p. 177. De Gaulle explicitly warned against forming Europe into an artificial motherland, the brainchild of the technocrats. De Gaulle, *Memoirs of Hope*, p. 183.

251 Konrad Adenauer had a special sense of belonging to the Greco-Roman-Christian heritage. This heritage referred to the Christian-humanist worldview, which included Western European Christianity and the Greco-Roman traditions of thought. Adenauer believed that antiquity (the ancient past especially the time before the middle ages) constitutes a wealth which he received

concerns expressed by the founding fathers regarding the elimination of the cultural roots of Europe in forming the European Union, proved to be legitimate. A mass culture, and even an anti-culture, currently replaces high culture, national cultures, and religion, in the Europe of today.

Categories of high culture, sovereignty, national cultures, and religion in Europe, were developed in a civilization that followed personalistic philosophies. These philosophies were based on the crystallization of the ultimate value and reality in persons, the concept the human being as a person. The triad of Truth, Goodness, and Beauty, dating back to ancient Greece, made up the main categories of European civilization. A human could fully develop as a person, when these qualities were preserved.

Christian cultural heritage defines the triad of truth, goodness, and beauty, as given to the human person by a supreme God, the God who is the creator and purpose of human life. God became known to humanity in Christian Europe, as the triad of Father, Son, and Holy Spirit. Whether remembered theoretically, or in relationship between a person and their God, Europe's cultural history includes this Christian dimension.

The concept of Europe within the European Union is being created in opposition to what makes Europe, to be Europe. The triad is ignored and

---

from his Christian heritage and culture. He believed certain fundamental ideas were transferred to him, ideas stemming from important characteristics belonging to Europe's heritage. These characteristics consist of human individual rights; human dignity; an understanding of the cosmos in the sense of an order filled with spirituality; fear of chaos; the ability to do what is necessary at the right time; and the ability to wait for the right time in order to do what is right. –*Enquête über die Rolle des griechisch-lateinischen Geisteserbes in der Bildungsgesellschaft von morgen*, WortundWahrheit, 1964, H. 1, p. 11. As cited in *Adenauer. Europa.* The whole text: 10 May 2018 http://www. konrad-adenauer.de/dokumente/artikel/artikel-wort-und-wahrheit. Adenauer "was imbued with the western culture which he understood to be a continuation of antiquity and Christianity. He was proficient in Latin until his old age and he used it in jokes when he spoke with clerks who wanted to work for him. He was able to confuse the majority of them. Latin was the expression of his understanding of education in a humanist sense." Jospeh Thesing, "Konrad Adenauer – życie i dzieło" [*Konrad Adenauer – Life and Work*], in: *Ojcowie współczesnej Europy. Materiały z konferencji* [*Fathers of the Contemporary Europe. Materials from Conferences*] (Warsaw: Kontrast, 1993), p. 36.

renounced both in the historical and cultural sense, and in the religious and moral sense. The European Union is made up of a technocratic system, a system whereby the power has shifted from elected representatives, to engineers, managers and scientists. This technocratic system is a system in which the political leaders behave as if they were technocrats (knowing everything about a subject). Their aim is to control society as if this society were a pure machine.

Christian Democracy was replaced by a version of socialism that was developed by the Frankfurt School as a form of left-wing ideology adapted for the West. The Frankfurt School in Germany was founded in 1923 for Marxist studies. When the process of European integration was started at the end of the Second World War, the Frankfurt School declared their commitment to the principles and aims of the European cultural tradition, especially Christianity. This commitment was negated through maneuvering. Manipulative strategies were implemented in such a way that the majority of Christian voters did not notice what was happening. The Christian Democratic Party was gradually lead by and controlled by socialism. Socialist ideologies were implemented in sensitive areas including morality and faith.[252]

Christian Democratic Europe in practice became a socialist Europe. A strong and consistent secularization program of Europe is being implemented. The Christian Democratic party has lost its roots and focus. It no longer holds fast and true to Christian religious and cultural principles. Christian morality no longer exists. Laws inconsistent with Christian morality are enacted. The implemented laws may hold true for those ascribing to a secularist worldview, but in terms of maintaining a European culture, they are devastating.

---

252 Knowledge about such a paradoxical and shocking situation is already available even in Wikipedia, where we may read that contemporary Christian Democrats are connected with Christianity, or even with religion, only a little: "the majority of large Christian Democratic parties established after World War II grew away from Catholic roots and adopted a supra-denominational character – party members include also persons belonging to non-Christian religions and non-believers. The contemporary Christian democracy is inspired by the principles of Christian ethics, but it gave up references to religion:" 10 May 2018 http://pl.wikipedia.org/wiki/Chrze%C5 %9Bcija%C5 %84ska_demokracja.

The secular world judges and condemns people who speak out against these practices. As Christians make up the majority of people who defend Christian principles, they are ostracized and condemned. Intimidation is used as a method of silencing opposition to this socialist worldview, in the form of threats, shame, ridicule, name calling (bigot), attacks against the person's intelligence (uneducated), and sometimes death.

Those who support views opposite to the current worldview, including Christians, are concerned because laws that do not preserve the dignity of life do not lead to love, family, personal unity, peace, contentment, joy, or truth. Instead these new laws enacted lead to division, strife, mental and physical health problems, and death. The Union was implemented to create peace and not division. Laws promoting life that are consistent with Christian beliefs, lead to peace, the initial and fundamental purpose of the creation of a European Union.

There were many factors to consider when the forefathers of the European Union first began to envision the benefits of a united Europe. These forefathers wanted most of all to work towards a Europe that would be prosperous and peaceful, and a Europe that would continue to maintain a culture that had been developing over centuries. Europe had been predominately Christian, encompassing a culture and peoples that adhered to Christian principles. Following the Christian model of behavior had ramifications in terms of religion, and also in terms of culture. When people practiced the Christian religion, people experienced peace, joy, fulfilment, love, and forgiveness. These were not qualities that lead to hostility and war. There has been no other religion in the history of time that allowed peace and harmony between nations to exist, such as was offered through Christian practices.

The concept of a united Europe developed within the context of the Christian religion, culture, and values. In the 1970's, the direction of the Union in terms of treaties, negotiations, and laws, began to turn to the left towards socialism. Initial fundamental principles were being eroded, even though proponents advocated that principles included were in fact Christian and that they embraced Christian democracy. The process of De – Christianization was done so skillfully, that in the Europe of today, Christianity is openly discriminated against. In place is a centrally controlled secularization process that uses education and the media to create mass brainwashing. This strategy has been so effective in turning Europe against Christianity that the quantity and quality of Christians in Europe is decreasing. Historically, an active persecution against Christians, such as that which occurred in Communist Russia, just served to increase the resolve of the people. In terms of the Union, an effective form of propaganda was the strategy used to conquer and combat Christianity. It used, and gradually eliminated, Christian values and ideals from treaties and agreements between nations. This program has proven to be more effective in eliminating Christianity in Europe, than has been persecution.

The numbers of Christians who really understand and who practice their faith declines. Less people in Europe have knowledge about their culture, civilization and about Europe. When comparing the effects of the loss of culture in other parts of the world, it is possible to document the devastation that has resulted in terms of the people being studied. Most are aware of aboriginal peoples of the world and the effects that culture loss has caused them as a people. In the case of Europe, because the deculturization process has been so skillfully maneuvered, people are not yet identifying the loss that ensues. Consider the example of a frog placed in a pot of water. A frog put in a pot of cold water will not know it is in danger as the pot is gradually heated to a boil. Because the frog doesn't know to save itself, it will die. The secularization of Europe is difficult to stop. People are not aware of the process being used to manipulate them away from their roots. For those who are being vigilant about what is happening, it is clear that the concept of Europe being developed through the European Union is a concept that is in opposition to Christianity. It particularly targets its opposition against the Catholic Church.[253] The dispute about fundamental principles and goals has taken the form of a battle, the battle for Europe. This battle sometimes has expanded to include intercontinental and sometimes intra-continental

---

253 Such a great struggle with Christianity, at least in the public sphere, is a response of left-wing circles to the diagnosis made by Antonio Gramsci, who believed that without the elimination of Christianity, the victory of Marxism is not possible. Today it is about the victory of Neo-Marxism. See Dalmacio Negro, *Lo que Europa debe al Cristianismo* (Madrid: Union Editorial S. A. 2004), p. 117.

nations. This battle has been taking place from the beginning. It is a battle connected with faith, and with civilization.

There is hope. The real Europe is worth saving. The Europe of the past, and of the future, has distinctiveness when compared with the civilizations of other continents. Europe can be faithful to the classical and Christian culture of the past. Europe can uphold the universal elements, those that value the dignity and worth of a person on all levels, as "MAN" (and woman), is discovered and affirmed as a person. This person has a role and value in the context of family, social, and religious life. Personalism, a theory that emphasizes human dignity and value, was developed in the European culture. This personalism must be defended by Europe, as it continues to define itself in the direction of a united Europe.

VIII. The End with No End

New Clashes: Geography, Religion, and No Religion

From the beginning of time, Europe has experienced clashes; it has been part of a battlefield. Clashes over Europe involved geography, culture, philosophy, religion, essential values, practices of living out life... the list is ongoing.

In ancient times, the Greeks referred to their conflict with Persia as a clash between Europe and Asia. Later, the clash was between Islam and Christianity. This clash was not about geography. The clash centered on religion, culture and civilization. Later, clashes centered on ideology and non-religion. Communism, Nazism, and Fascism, took their tole on Europe in more recent years. In our current generation, the clash is subtle, perhaps not perceived by the people, as being any source of threat.

Europe's Journey, A New Beginning

Europe's journey could have started in various time periods, with key poets and philosophers, including Homer, or in the time of Descartes, Newton or Marx. Europe could have begun with the strong political structures of ancient Greece or ancient Rome. Europe could also have begun with medieval Christianity, with the new ideas concerning the human being, the family and society. Each of these time periods witnessed clashes, historical events that needed resolution.

The New Losses: Identity, History, Civilization

After surviving conflicts and clashes throughout the generations, Europe is now faced with new types of problems. These problems include identity, history, and basic aims. Europe has lost its sense of identity. Identity is about one's uniqueness, one's character, and one's civilization. It is about what makes Europe to be Europe. Identity is related to one's history of civilization, its advanced stage of social development, and its complex legal, political, and religious organization. Every person needs to be aware of and be familiar with one's own cultural heritage, which serves to form ones cultural and social identity. This identity leads to a sense of belonging, of being part of the broader social and cultural context. A civilization can be lost, when structural elements of its cultural identity deteriorate. These elements include, for example, activities, customs, values, tradition, education, religion, language, and collective memories, the combination of which shape the people who live there. These elements serve to form a social cohesion. Collective memories are memories that have been passed on from previous generations, historically, molding a person's personality, helping a person to discover meaning in the surrounding world.

European history envelops crucial events, and the methods in which the European culture responded and adapted to those events. History encompasses all that is essential, allowing Europe and Europeans to be different, to be unique, to be special. Historical events allowed Europe to begin to be Europe, and then to follow a path, a way, that could only be European. Basic aims and objectives can only be implemented when clearly defined. Historically: European aims are in the realm of culture and its spiritual dimension, not though the means of technology, production and economy.

Europe has been a source of paradox. Throughout history, there seem to be so many different Europe's. One wonders whether there also have been some true, and some false Europe's. European history has embodied an internal struggle. Some of this internal struggle may have had some external inspiration. True to history, Europe is currently struggling. It is not struggling as it did in the past, because of geography, politics and culture. The struggle now, is about civilization.

Economic Challenges and Political Harmony

Following the Second World War, Europe experienced a split between two strong and opposing political systems: Capitalist and Communist. Potential hostilities served as a great threat to peace. Europe had just experienced the devastation of two world wars. Preventing a third war was high as a European priority. Christian leaders proposed a united Europe as a solution to the growing threats. Cooperation seemed to be a better solution, than the potential collapse that would result from confrontation. A series of treaties ensued, in order to create a united and peaceful Europe. Turning points of European history continue, as history continues to unfold. This newest turning point in European history embraces the idea of Europe being united into one Europe, The United Europe has been termed: the European Union, the E.U.

Europe United and Strong?

The goals of a united Europe that were initially formulated through the leaders of various European countries, included: fellowship, peaceful human relationships, and the valuing of all human life, which, it was hoped, would inevitably lead to world peace. Initially, the Union embraced the heritage of classic culture, classical philosophy, and Christianity. A classical Christian culture is a culture that has been nourished with both the ancient Greek and ancient Roman cultures. Ancient culture had a place in the development of Europe.

The Ancient Greeks invented and discovered classical philosophy. The Greeks attempted to intellectually grasp the concept of reality. The Greeks wanted to understand what reality is and to understand why reality is real. Non-classical philosophies lost the main object or aim. They saw reality as being ideal. They aimed to know how, rather than to know why. European culture valued its ability to consider concepts, and examine these concepts in terms of their deeper significance to the human race.

A peaceful society based upon classical philosophy, may not be an answer. There is nothing wrong with its aims. However, we have to look at the real situation that encompasses the human being, and society in this world. This real situation too often implemented, is one of wars and fights. Then, one may wonder: Who is trustful? Soviets in the name of peace enslaved many nations and killed millions. We should not be too naïve. Peace is the end; peace is what we are striving for. Peace is not the beginning.

Christian doctrine attempted to explain the perpetuity that the human being has for conflict and war. Christian scripture tells of a story at the beginning of creation. Satan seduced Eve and Adam to disobey God. Adam and Eve lost their place in the Garden of Eden, the relationship they had with God, and they lost their innocence. They lost the ability to live in a paradise. They lost their ability to live in a way, whereby they knew not to choose evil. It was, according to Biblical Revelation, the beginning of all future conflicts and wars.

Classical philosophy will not explain difficulties in terms of scripture or revelation, in terms of Classical theology. Classical philosophy tries to explain the reasons that it is so hard to achieve a peace, not only in the society, but also even in the small family. When, in our current society, there is difficulty successfully curing the family, how might the big society be cured? In reality it is difficult. Classical philosophy tries to explain the reasons that peace is so difficult to achieve.

Could Europe strive towards a religion and philosophy of peace as a means of managing current difficulties? No, because this statement is too ambiguous and too large. There can be other religions of peace. As for philosophy, this would not be strictly philosophy, to be understood in a classical way. The objective is to keep a classical understanding of philosophy, a theoretical, and not a practical wisdom. One can build a model of a peaceful society that is based upon classical philosophy, but it is closer to utopia. A return to Christianity, perhaps starting with a return to the values that embrace the Christian faith, has been suggested as a means to solve the current European difficulties.

The goals of the Union were commendable. However, these initial goals and objectives have become displaced. Some non-European civilizations may be creating an influence indirectly, while hiding behind European forms.

Europe remembered the ideologies of Nazism, Fascism, Socialism, and Communism. These ideologies lead to bloody revolutions. As time progressed, the European Union changed its opponent, aiming its focus against Christianity. A new clash over Europe began to emerge. Gone were the ideologies that aimed to preserve a culture rich in heritage and history.

Europe Displacing Religion

Unfortunately, Europe is beginning to follow a new path. The European Union is becoming more and more atheistic, and more secularized. In the name of tolerance, the European Union is undertaking a game with Islam. This movement against Christianity, is very dangerous, not only for the Church but for the European Union itself.

The true western concept of nationality has been solidly grounded upon cultural and moral values. The historical ideal of a nation, and there have been many in Europe, at one time held its history and culture in the highest of esteem.

At the end of the eighteenth century, during the time of the French Revolution, the idea of a continuous nation was replaced by the idea of citizenship. This citizenship was based solely upon administrative criteria. Administrative criteria make the human life void of deeper values and ideals. Atheism and "Cosmo" or "Europolitics" cannot solve the problem of the decadence and nihilism corroding the European Union. Europolitics is an information system that was implemented to provide a critical analysis of policies, decisions, and initiatives of the European Union, and the institutions that affect business and its citizens. Europolitics keeps decision makers informed about the decision making processes affecting European Law. The value of a nation, once based upon a thorough grounding in a rich cultural heritage, is being eroded.

Where Is Europe Going?

When examining European civilization and culture from an historical reference, one thing is certain: Contemporary Europe, in the form of the European Union, promotes the development of a new Europe which is not in agreement with Europeanism in terms of history and civilization. This new concept of Europe is moving towards the ideology of socialism. Socialism leading to Communism has been detrimental to Europe. Communism did fail in Russian history. The new European identity, established through the European Union, is built upon the pillars of socialism. It views its largest enemy to be Christianity, as did Communism in Russia, and Nazism in Germany. This socialism of the European Union, denies the Greco – Roman heritage of Europe and its Christian foundation, the pillars upon which Europe was built. Europe was built as a unique phenomenon in the history of the world. Now, one may envision an increasingly inflamed fight of Europe against Europe.

In the socialistic current practice of Europe, it has lost the ideas that were central to European heritage. It has lost the idea of a human being as being a person. The family has no significance. Gone is the idea of the family as being a monogenic relation based upon stable love and fidelity, between a mother and a father, and between parents and children. Europe is losing the

identity of being a national and religious society. If Europe loses awareness
of its uniqueness in these areas, Europe will be able to produce and trade
more and more. Europe, at the same time, will strengthen other civilizations
that would be ready to conquer Europe. European generations are made
defenseless. European generations would not be available to follow the
European traditions and would not have a culture. Contemporary European
civilization is broken. The critical problem Europe is now facing, is about
how might Europe be able to recover its own coherent civilization.

Attempting to Resolve Economical Problems

Europe is attempting to resolve its crucial problems on the basis
of economy. Europe is attempting to substitute religion (especially
Christianity) and high culture, with mass culture and ideology. This is
an impossible goal. Economy as economy is concerned with the means
only. Economy cannot generate the real ends. The source of ideology is
the human mind, of human thought. Mass media too easily can succumb
to propaganda. Propaganda cannot be a substitute for the truth, even
if has been repeated millions of times, and in a pleasant way. Religion
has its roots in reality, coming from the existential experience of every
human being. Its expressions can be different, and that is the reason for
the prevalence of so many religions. Religion is an answer to experience.
Human experience enters deeply into the core of reality, and also into
the ultimate meaning of human life. Human life is different from the life
of any creature on this Earth. Any civilization without religion is on a
straight path towards committing suicide.

The Attractiveness of Europe

Europe maintains some very positive qualities, in spite of current difficulties.
Europe remains attractive due to its openness to and reverence towards very
rich and different traditions and cultures. Europe is not homogeneous. There
are many divergent and rich European cultures. A list of each European
country would be too exhaustive an exercise. Listing a small select portion
of these serves for illustration only. Some of these cultures, to name a few,
include the British, Croatian, Dutch, French, German, Hungarian, Italian,
Polish, Portuguese, Russian, and Spanish cultures. As we list some of these

European countries, we get a vast sense of a unique and diversified Europe, rich in a cultural heritage that cannot be measured.

These cultures can co-exist in harmony if all these varied cultures and traditions are grounded in, or at least respect their roots. Countries, including Britain, France, Italy, Poland, Portugal, and Spain, may respect the roots of their Latin civilization.

Europe's Clash of Civilizations: What Is Next?

Europe is experiencing a clash of civilizations, a new fight over Europe. This fight remains below the surface, and unless examined with critical thinking, will remain unnoticed to the casual observer. No one knows how this clash will end. This clash weakens Europe. Compromise is difficult if not impossible. The wide range of contradicting and incompatible rules interfere with its progress. Arguments used currently may refer to utopia, and or, ideology. Striving towards utopia is extremely dangerous. Utopia is an intellectual project, which, in the name of happiness, does not respect a real human being, and or, its needs. To achieve its ends, utopia treats a real human being as an object of manipulation, deformation or even annihilation. In the name of communist utopia there were around one hundred million, to one hundred and fifty million people killed. The Black Book of Communism provides the historical details.[254] Utopia does not respect reality as reality. Utopia does not respect a human being, as being a real being. Utopia does not treat a person as a subject, but instead treats the person as an object. This list could be continued. Striving for utopia, it is so dangerous.

Arguments would be better focused upon facts. Facts and historical examination form reliable sources of truth about Europe. Based upon historical details as presented previously in this book, Europe is doomed to collapse without the inclusion of the heritage of classic and Christian culture.

In terms of a philosophy, and a religion that would most likely generate world peace, world leaders over the centuries, chose to include Christianity.

---

254 *The Black Book of Communism: Crimes, Terror, Repression* (Cambridge; London: Harvard University Press, 1999).

This religion and behavioral practice provided some countries with centuries of success and peace. If we want to survive as a world, the return of Christian values and practices, to classical philosophy and the inclusion of a Christian religion, may be the only option for Europe. It would be advantageous for Europe to allow and promote the Christian culture, developed over the centuries, to continue to exist.

The many cultures of Europe could continue to coexist in harmony, if all the varied cultures and traditions of Europe would be grounded in or at least respect their roots, the Latin civilization. The Latin civilization gave as its central idea, a person, not a nation, a state, a group of believers, or even an individual. A person represents personalism. Personalism demands respect for every human being as a subject, endowed with dignity. The human is not viewed as an object, nor as a divine end, and not as a means. If the truths about the dignity of a person are not respected, Europe will eventually collapse.

Europe has collapsed many times in its history. Most recently, Europe collapsed due to two world wars. Europe was able to revive. It revived due to its ability to recall Christian teaching based upon Personalism and fundamental human rights.

Through suggesting a return to Christianity, it does not imply that all Europeans would be forced to be Christians. When a religion becomes forced, free choice is compromised, which is anti-Christian. In history, the Byzantine civilization forced religion upon its subjects. An attempt to force Christianity would imply a change of civilization, from Latin to Byzantine. What Europe really needs now is its Latin civilization, which enables Europe to flourish and to be a source of true values not only for Europeans, but also for all humanity.

One may wonder whether an atheist society that strives to create peace and harmony and Christian values, would be preferable to a society that is Christian and fighting. Examples cited for the sake of argument include Ireland's protestant and catholic fights; Muslims fighting; Ku Klux Klan killings; or the witch burning that occurred in Christian history. This argument can be refuted by Christian theology.

The basic Christian value is a value based upon a belief and relationship with a supreme God, and this relationship is love. The Christian Bible tells of the Christian perspective about love, as written in the form of a letter, written by Saint Paul. In this text, any action, sacrifice, any power, and any knowledge without love is nothing.[255]

According to a Christian belief system, atheists cannot strive towards real peace and happiness without loving God. Atheists remove what is the most essential, which is and can only be God. Conflicts and wars come not from religion itself but from erroneous theology (interpretations of what Revelation says) or from the evil will. According to Christian theology, these vices are all effects of the original sin, as committed by Adam and Eve when they first disobeyed God.

Could universal Christianity save Europe, based on the historical reference of the Christian culture that Europe grew on, that made Europe Unique? Can we assume that, what worked in the past, could be a solution for the future? There are some basic values and principles, which we have to respect. There are still many different roads one can follow now and in the future. The basic value as proposed by Christians, is the conception of the human being, as being a person. The notion of a human being as being a person, appears only in Christianity. A human being, to be respected in the order of politics, economy, education, and health care, can be respected in many domains. There are no detailed rules about how to achieve this value of human dignity. It is always open to negation. We are always free.

In terms of Christianity, as a religion, the faithful ask for God's assistance to live according to Christian values, which include: education, hospitals, care of poor, and forgiveness. Those practices are not unique to Christianity. Many faiths, embrace these practices, including Muslims. All religions have extremists.

---

255 This passage gives instruction about the qualities of love. "Love is patient; love is kind; love is not envious or boastful or arrogant or rude. It does not insist on its own way; it is not irritable or resentful; it does not rejoice in wrongdoing, but rejoices in the truth. It bears all things, believes all things, hopes all things, endures all things. Love never ends. But as for prophecies, they will come to an end; as for tongues, they will cease; as for knowledge, it will come to an end" 1 Corinthians 13: 4–8 *the New Revised Standard Version Bible, Catholic Edition (NRSVCE)*, copyright © 1989, 1993 the Division of Christian Education of the National Council of the Churches of Christ in the United States of America. Used by permission. All rights reserved: https://www.biblegateway.com/theN ewRevisedStandardVersionBible/CatholicEdition (RESVCE).

If Europe was to embrace a religion, one may wonder why Europe would embrace Christianity, when there are so many other faiths to choose from? Why would Europe not embrace a defined faith (a community of people who love and care for each other) that does not have a religious label? Embracing the Christian faith could be preferable to embracing the Muslim faith. Europe is based upon a history of Christianity, which honors its deep cultural roots. Specifically, with regards to the Muslim faith, there are places in the Koran about jihad, "kill those who do not follow your religion." To kill those who are not Muslim is not the extremist view of Islam, it is written in the Koran itself. Let's start from this point our discussion. Nowhere in the Christian Bible does it suggest to kill the opposition. Instead, it discusses acceptance of people, peace, harmony, reconciliation, and love. In the New Testament it is even said to love your enemy.

Apologetics strive toward creating conversion in hearts, and to provide teachings towards that end. Christian apologetics would be a process aimed to assist people to convert to Christianity. Muslim apologetics would strive towards converting people to Islam.

This work is not apologetics. Apologetics means that it is a point of departure (a religious truth). One does not manipulate with philosophy. This book is written at the level of the philosophy of culture, not religion as such, but religion is a part of culture. The universal meaning of Christianity is a viable proposal to save Europe. Europe has fallen in the past. Europe has hope of revival. Europe needs to return to a source of true values based upon personalism and human rights. Europe needs to return to its roots, its history, and its culture. Europe needs to heal its current very large wound, and be made whole again. A healthy Europe is possible to achieve. It can be done. The future is filled with hope.

Bibliography

Aristotle. *Politics*. Trans. Benjamin Jowett. Oxford: Clarendon Press, 1885.

Aristotle. *Rhetoric*. Trans. William Rhys Roberts. Oxford: Clarendon Press, 1924.

Aristotle. *Metaphysics*. Trans. William David. Ross. Oxford: Clarendon, 1928.

Barrio, Jaime F. „Europa en el pensamiento de Jaspers," *Pensamiento. Revista de investigación e información filosófica*, Vol. 53, No. 205, 1997.

Blaut, James M. *Eight Eurocentric Historians*. New York; London: Guilford Press, 2000.

Bokajło, Wiesław. *Koncepcja Europy Konrada Adenauera i jej realizacja w praktyce politycznej w latach 1945–1954 [The Idea of Europe According to Konrad Adenauer and its Realization in Political Practice in the Years 1945–1954]*. Wrocław: Wydawnictwo Uniwersytetu Wrocławskiego, 1995.

Brosch, Pius. *Die Ontologie des Johannes Clauberg*. Greifswald: Druck von E. Hartmann, 1926.

Burnet, John. *Early Greek Philosophy*. London: Methuen and Co., 1930.

Buttiglione, Rocco and Jarosław Merecki. *Europa jako pojęcie filozoficzne, [Europe as a Philosophical Concept]*. Lublin: Towarzystwo Naukowe KUL, 1996.

Carpentier, Jean. "L'Europe, le mot et le space." In: *Histoire de l'Europe*, ed. Jean Carpentier and François Lebrun. Paris: Édition du Seuil, 1992.

Curtius, Quintus. *History of Alexander*. Trans. John C. Rolfe. Cambridge: Harvard University Press, 2006.

Czuba, Krystyna. *Idea Europy kultur w nauczaniu Jana Pawła II [Concept of Europe of Cultures in the Teachings of John Paul II]*. Warsaw: Wydawnictwo Soli Deo, 2003.

Dawson, Christopher. "Europe and the Seven Stages of Western Culture." In: *Christianity and European Culture. Selections from the Work of Christopher Dawson*, ed. Gerald J. Russello. Washington: Catholic University of America Press, 1998.

Dawson, Christopher. *The Making of Europe. An Introduction to the History of European Unity*. Washington DC: The Catholic University of America Press, 2003.

Frye, Richard N. *La herencia de Persia*. Madrid: Ediciones Guardarrama, 1965.

Gaudefroy-Demombynes, Maurice. *Mahomet. L'homme et son message*. Paris: Albin, 1957.

Goberna Faique, Juan R. *Civilización. Historia de una idea*. Santiago de Compostela: Universidad de Santiago de Compostela. Servicio de Publicacións e Intercambio Cientifico, 1999.

Graves, Robert. *The Greek Myths*. Baltimore: Penguine Books, 1955.

Hartog, Francois. "Fondamenti greci dell'idea d'Europa." In: *Idee di Europa. Attualità e fragilità di un progetto antico*, ed. Luciano Canfora. Bari: Dedalo, 1997.

Hippocrates, "Influences of Atmosphere, Water and Situation," *Greek Historical Thought from Homer to the Age of Heraclius*. Trans. Arnold J. Toynbee. Boston: Beacon Press, 1950.

I fondatori del Europa Unita secondo il progetto di Jean Monnet, Robert Schuman, Konrad Adenauer, Alcide de Gasperi. Cantalupa: Effatà Editrice, 1999.

Im Hof, Ulrich. *Europa der Aufklärung*. München: Beck, 1993.

Isocrates. Trans. George Norlin. Cambridge; London: Harvard University Press, 1991.

Jaeger, Werner. *Paideia. The Ideals of Greek Culture*. Vol. 1. Oxford: Basil Blackwell, 1946.

Jareño Alarcón, Jaquín. "Identidad y ciudadanía en la nueva Europa. Algunos motivos para reflexión." In: *Miradas sobre Europa*, eds. Joaquín Jareño Alarcón, Miguel Ángel García Olmo. Murcia: Fundación Universitaria San Antonio, 2006.

Jaroszyński, Piotr. *Człowiek i nauka. Studium z filozofii kultury [Man and Science. Studies in the Philosophy of Culture]*. Lublin: Polskie Towarzystwo Tomasza z Akwinu, 2008.

Jaroszyński, Piotr. *Metaphysics or Ontology?* Trans. Hugh McDonald. Leiden and Boston: Brill and Rodopi, 2018.

Jaskólska, Julia. "Powody i okoliczności proklamowania Powszechnej Deklaracji Praw Człowieka [Reasons and Circumstances of Proclaiming the Universal Declaration of Human Rights]." *Człowiek w kulturze [Man in Culture]*, Vol. 11. Lublin: Polskie Towarzystwo Tomasza z Akwinu, 1998.

Kościelniak, Krzysztof. *Dżihad. Święta wojna w islamie [Jihad. Holy war in Islam]*. Kraków: Wydawnictwo "M", 2002.

Krąpiec, Mieczyław A. *Metaphysics. An Outline of the Theory of Being*. New York: Peter Lang, 1991.

Krąpiec, Mieczysław A. *Filozofia w teologii [Philosophy in Theology]*. Lublin: Instytut Edukacji Narodowej, 1999.

Lysias. Trans. William R.M. Lamb. Cambridge: Harvard University Press; London: William Heinemann Ltd. 1930.

Maritain, Jacques. *Three Reformers. Luther, Descartes Rousseau*. London: Sheed and Ward, 1950.

Messori, Vittorio. *Czarne karty Kościoła [Black Pages of the Church]*. Trans. Antoni Kajzerek. Katowice: Księgarnia św. Jacka, 1998.

Moore, Jerry D. "Franz Boas. Culture in Context." In: Visions of Culture. An Introduction to Anthropological Theories and Theorists, ed. Jerry D. More. California: AltaMira Press, 1997.

Negro, Dalmacio. *Lo que Europa debe al Cristianismo*. Madrid: Union Editorial S. A. 2004.

Nisbet, Robert. *Historia de la idea de progreso*. Barcelona: España, 1981.

Nowak, Jerzy R. *Kościół a Rewolucja Francuska [The Church and the French Revolution]*. Szczecinek: Fundacja Nasza Przyszłość, 1999.

Peeters, Marguerite A. *Le gender: une norme politique et culturelle mondiale. Outil de discernement*. Paris: Mame, 2012.

Poppinga, Anneliese. "O osobowości Konrada Adenauera. Polityk i chrześcijanin" [On the Personality of Konrad Adenauer. A Politician and a Christian]. *Konrad Adenauer. Europa chrześcijańska. Christliches Europa, Documentation of Polish and German scientific on 15th and 16th December 1994*. Lublin: Towarzystwo Naukowe Katolickiego Uniwersytetu Lubelskiego: Fundacja Rozwoju KUL, 1995.

Reale, Giovanni. *Raíces culturales y espirituales de Europa. Por un renacimiento de 'hombre europeo'*. Trans. Maria Pons Irazazábal. Madrid: Herder Editorial, 2005.

Roman, Luke and Monica Roman. *Encyclopedia of Greek and Roman Mythology*. New York: Infobase Publishing, 2010.

Rossi, Paolo. *Francis Bacon. From Magic to Science*.Trans. Sacha
Rabinovitch, Chicago: University of Chicago Press, 1978.

Rozwadowski, Władysław. *Prawo rzymskie. Zarys wykładu wraz z
wyborem źródeł [Roman Law]*, Warszawa: Wydawnictwo Naukowe
PWN, 1991.

Secher, Reynald. *Le Génocide franco-français – La Vendée-Vengé*. Paris:
Presses Universitaires de France, 1986.

Sierra Gonzáles, Angela. "El constitucionalismo fallido de la Unión
Europea." *Europa a examen. Nuevo diálogos sobre el Viejo Mundo.*
Madrid: Editorial Dykinsen, 2013.

Sugar, Peter F. "Fascism and Nationalism." *Encyclopedia of Nationalism.*
San Diego; San Francisco: Academic Press, 2001.

Tarasiewicz, Paweł. "Jan Paweł II o totalitaryzmie" [John Paul II on
Totaltarianism] *Totalitaryzm: jawny czy ukryty? [Totalitarianism:
Open or Hidden?]*. Lublin: Lubelska Szkoła Filozofii Chrześcijańskiej,
2011.

The Holy Bible. Kings James Version. Peabody: Hendrickson Publishers,
2014.

The Homeric Hymns. Trans. Apostolos N. Athanassakis. Baltimore;
London: John Hopkins University Press, 2004, 2nd ed.

Weber, Max. *The Protestant Ethics and the Spirit of Capitalism.* Trans.
Talcott Parsons. London; New York: Routledge, 2005.

Wilson, Kevin and Jan van der Dussen. *History of the Idea of Europe.*
London; New York: Routledge, 1995.

Wladimiri, Paul. *Works of Paul Wladimiri. A Selection.* ed. Ludwik
Ehrlich (Warszawa: Instytut Wydawniczy PAX, 1968), 3 volumes.

Władysław, Tatarkiewicz, *Historia filozofii [History of Philosophy].* Vol. 1.
Warszawa: Państwowe Wydawnictwo Naukowe, 1970.

Wriedt, Markus. "Luther's Theology." *The Cambridge Companion to
Luther*. New York: Cambridge University Press, 2003.

Zdybicka, Zofia J. *Partycypacja bytu. Próba wyjaśnienia relacji między
światem i Bogiem [Participation of Being. An Attempt to Explain
the Relation Between the World and God]*. Lublin: Towarzystwo
Naukowe KUL, 1972.

Internet Sources

"450 B.C. – The World According to Herodotus." https://www. awesomestories.com/asset/view/450-B.C.-The-World-According-to-Herodotus/ (2 May 2018)

"Boundaries." https://en.wikipedia.org/wiki/Boundaries_between_ continents/ (26 May 2018)

ClaritasU: https://claritasu.com/courses.

"Chrześcijańska demokracja [Christian Democracy]." Wikipedia. http:// pl.wikipedia.org/wiki/Chrze%C5 %9Bcija%C5 %84ska_demokracja/ (26 May 2018)

Euthanasia Deception: https://youtube.com/euthanasiadeception.

Holy Bible: https:// www.biblegateway.com: *[Scripture quotations are]*from the New Revised Standard Version Bible: Catholic Edition, copyright © 1989, 1993 the Division of Christian Education of the National Council of the Churches of Christ in the United States of America. Used by permission. All rights reserved.

"Homily of his Eminence Card. Joseph Ratzinger Dean of the College of Cardinals." Vatican, 18 April, 2005. http://www.vatican.va/gpII/ documents/homily-pro-eligendo-pontifice_20050418_en.html/ (26 May 2018)

"Isidori Hispalensis episcopi Etymologiarum sive originum libri XX." http://www.thelatinlibrary.com/isidore/14.shtml/ (2 May 2018)

"Mainstreaming Gender in the European Union – Jean Monnet Center." www.jeanmonnetprogram.org/archive/papers/00/000201.rtf/ (26 May 2018)

Post abortion syndrome: https://www.afterabortion.com/quiz.

Prolife: https://www.prolife.com.

"Robert Schuman on Democracy." http://users.belgacombusiness.net/ schuman/democracy.htm/ (26 May 2018)

"The Schuman Declaration. 9 May 1950." http://europa.eu/about-eu/ basic-information/symbols/europe-day/schuman-declaration/index_ en.htm/ (26 May 2018)

"Thomas Aquinas – Moral Philosophy." Internet Encyclopedia of
    Philosophy. http://www.iep.utm.edu/aq-moral/ (26 May 2018)

"Universal Declaration of Human Rights." http://www.un.org/en/
    universal-declaration-human-rights/ (26 May 2018)

Adenauer, Konrad. "Anfang 1964: Über die Rolle des griechisch-
    lateinischen Geisteserbes in der Bildungsgesellschaft von morgen."
    http://www.konrad-adenauer.de/dokumente/artikel/artikel-wort-und-
    wahrheit/ (26 May 2018)

Adenauer, Konrad. "Staatsauffasung. Bonn 7.04.1946." https://www.
    konrad-adenauer.de/biographie/zitate/staatsauffassung/ (26 May 2018)

Aristotle. "Metaphysics." Trans. William D. Ross. http://classics.mit.edu/
    Aristotle/metaphysics.html/ (26 May 2018)

Aristotle. "Politics." Trans. Benijamin Jowett. //classics.mit.edu/Aristotle/
    politics.7.seven.html/ (26 May 2018)

Aquinas, Thomas. "Scriptum Super Sententiis." http://www.
    corpusthomisticum.org/snp1001.html/ (26 May 2018)

Aquinas, Thomas. "Summa Theologica." http://www.
    corpuSummaTheologicaomisticum.org/iopera.html/ (26 May 2018)

Alar, Fr Chris, *Devine Mercy 101*. https://www.devinemercy.org.

Baur, Erwin, Eugen Fischer and Fritz Lenz. "Grundriss der menschlichen
    Erblichkeitslehre und Rassenhygiene." München: J. F. Lehmanns Verlag,
    1921. https://archive.org/details/grundrissdermens02bauruoft (5 May 2018)

Benedict XVI. "Faith, Reason and the University. Memories and
    Reflections." University of Regensburg 12 Sept, 2006. https://
    w2.vatican.va/content/benedict-xvi/en/speeches/2006/september/
    documents/hf_ben-xvi_spe_20060912_university-regensburg.html/ (26
    May 2018)

Chesterton, Gilbert K. "What's Wrong with the World." https://www.
    chesterton.org/wrong-with-world/ (26 May 2018)

Condorcet, Marie-Jean-Antoine-Nicolas Caritat, Marquis de. "Outlines
    of a Historical View of the Progress of the Human Mind, Being a
    Posthumous Work of the Late M. de Condorcet." Philadelphia: M.
    Carey, 1796. http://oll.libertyfund.org/titles/1669/ (26 May 2018)

John Paul II. "Address of His Holiness John Paul II at the Meeting of
    the Presbytery of Europe of the Church of Scotland, 7 March 1992."

https://w2.vatican.va/content/john-paul-ii/en/speeches/1992/march/
documents/hf_jp-ii_spe_19920307_presbiterio-scozia.html/ (26 May
2018)

John Paul II. "Address of His Holiness Pope John Paul II to the Former
Stagiaires of the Robert Schuman Foundation, 7.11.2003." https://
w2.vatican.va/content/john-paul-ii/en/speeches/2003/november/
documents/hf_jp-ii_spe_20031107_robert-schuman.html/ (26 May 2018)

John Paul II. "Discorso di Giovanni Paolo II agli studiosi europei
partecipanti al simposio presinodale su 'Cristianesimo e cultura in
Europa'". http://w2.vatican.va/content/john-paul-ii/it/speeches/1991/
october/documents/hf_jp-ii_spe_19911031_studiosi-europei.html (28
May 2018)

John Paul II. "Encyclical Letter Fides et ratio of the Supreme Pontiff John
Paul II to the Bishops of the Catholic Church on the Relationship
Between Faith and Reason." http://w2.vatican.va/content/john-paul-ii/
en/encyclicals/documents/hf_jp-ii_enc_14091998_fides-et-ratio.html/ (26
May 2018)

Kant, Immanuel. "The Critic of Practical Reason." Trans. Thomas
Kingsmill Abbott (Project Gutenberg). http://www.gutenberg.org/
ebooks/5683/ (26 May 2018)

Koneczny, Felix. "On the Plurality of Civilizations." London: Polonica
Publications, 1962. https://pl.scribd.com/doc/4464979/ON-THE-
PLURALITY-OF-CIVILIZATIONS-Feliks-Koneczny-Entire-Book/ (26
May 2018).

Lewis, Clive S. "God in the Dock." http://www.notable-quotes.com/l/
lewis_c_s.html/ (26 May 2018)

Lewis, Clive S. "Mere Christianity." https://www.goodreads.com/
quotes/99392-no-man-knows-how-bad-he-is-till-he-has/ (26 May 2018)

Maro, Publius V. "Aeneid." Trans. John Dryden. Perseus Digital Library.
http://www.perseus.tufts.edu/hopper/text?doc=Perseus%3Atext
%3A1999.02.0052 %3Abook%3D6 %3Acard%3D801/ (26 May
2018)

Montesquieu. "On the Spirit of the Laws." New York: The Colonial Press,
1899. https://archive.org/details/spiritoflaws01montuoft/ (26 May 2018)

Moschus. "Europe." http://www.theoi.com/Text/Moschus.html/ (2 May
2018)

Mother Theresa of Calcuta. http://www.vatican.va/roman_curia/
congregations/cevang/p_missionary_works/infantia/documents/rc_ic_
infantia_doc_20090324_boletin13p14_en.html/ (26 May 2018)

Niskanen, William A. "Comparing the U.S. and EU Constitutions." http://
www.cato.org/publications/commentary/comparing-us-eu-constitutions/
(26 May 2018)

Online Etymology Dictionary. https://www.etymonline.com/word/Europe/
(26 May 2018)

Ovid. "Metamorphoses". Trans. Stanley Lombardo. Indianapolis;
Cambridge: Hackett Publishing Company, Inc, 2010 7, 20: https://
books.google.pl/books?id=mwMLFWjHpQIC&printsec=frontcover&d
q=ovid+metamorphoses&hl=pl&sa=X&ved=0ahUKEwjwoNSEzevaAh
WLZVAKHS9AB4QQ6AEIJzAA#v=onepage&q&f=false (4 May 2018)

Rachel's Vineyard: https://www.rachelsvineyard.org.

Thucydides. "The History of the Peloponnesian War." Trans. Richard
Crawley. http://www.gutenberg.org/files/7142/7142-h/7142-h.
htm#link2H_4_0007/ (26 May 2018)

Madden, Thomas: "Understanding the Crusades".https://www.
lighthousecatholicmedia.org.

Weber, Max. "The Protestant Ethics and the Spirit of Capitalism."
Trans. Talcott Parsons. London; New York: Routledge, 2005. https://
is.muni.cz/el/1423/podzim2013/SOC571E/um/_Routledge_Classics___
Max_Weber-The_Protestant_Ethic_and_the_Spirit_of_Capitalism__
Routledge_Classics_-Routledge__2001_pdf/ (26 May 2018)

Studies in Politics, Security and Society

Edited by Stanisław Sulowski

www.peterlang.com